What Time Is It?

What Time Is It?

Marie B. Miller

VANTAGE PRESS
New York • Los Angeles

FIRST EDITION

All rights reserved, including the right of
reproduction in whole or in part in any form.

Copyright © 1991 by Marie B. Miller

Excerpts reprinted by kind permission of the *Birmingham Post-Herald*, and of Halley's Bible Handbook (Copyright © 1965 by Halley's Bible Handbook. Reprinted by permission.)

Published by Vantage Press, Inc.
516 West 34th Street, New York, New York 10001

Manufactured in the United States of America
ISBN: 0-533-09222-1

Library of Congress Catalog Card No.: 90-090247

1 2 3 4 5 6 7 8 9 0

*To all
who are watching and waiting
for the coming of
our Lord*

Contents

Acknowledgments	ix
Abbreviations from the King James Bible	xi
Introduction	1
Trumpets	12
The First Trumpet	18
The Second Trumpet	32
The Third Trumpet	75
The Fourth Trumpet	112
Let Us Ever Walk	123
Epilogue	125

Acknowledgments

I extend deep appreciation to all the special people who reviewed *What Time Is It?* and offered their comments and to Ernest Millen and Elfrieda Stueckler for the special preparation that made the manuscript ready for presentation and the patient care given to me in the evening of my life.

Abbreviations from the King James Bible

Books of the Old Testament	Abbreviation	Books of the New Testament	Abbreviation
Genesis	GEN	Matthew	MAT
Exodus	EXO	Mark	MAR
Leviticus	LEV	Luke	LUK
Numbers	NUM	John	JOH
Deuteronomy	DEU	The Acts	ACT
Joshua	JOS	Epistle to Romans	ROM
Judges	JDG	1 Corinthians	1CO
Ruth	RTH	2 Corinthians	2CO
1 Samuel	1SA	Galatians	GAL
2 Samuel	2SA	Ephesians	EPH
1 Kings	1KI	Philippians	PHI
2 Kings	2KI	Colossians	COL
1 Chronicles	1CH	1 Thessalonians	1TH
2 Chronicles	2CH	2 Thessalonians	2TH
Ezra	EZR	1 Timothy	1TI
Nehemiah	NEH	2 Timothy	2TI
Esther	EST	Titus	TIT
Job	JOB	Philemon	RHM
Psalms	PSA	Hebrews	HEB
Proverbs	PRO	Epistle of James	JAM
Ecclesiastes	ECC	1 Peter	1PE
Song of Solomon	SON	2 Peter	2PE
Isaiah	ISA	1 John	1JO

Books of the Old Testament	Abbreviation	Books of the New Testament	Abbreviation
Jeremiah	JER	2 John	2JO
Lamentations	LAM	3 John	3JO
Ezekiel	EZE	Jude	JUD
Daniel	DAN	Revelation	REV
Hosea	HOS		
Joel	JOE		
Amos	AMO		
Obadiah	OBA		
Jonah	JON		
Micah	MIC		
Nahum	NAH		
Habakkuk	HAB		
Zephaniah	ZEP		
Haggai	HAG		
Zechariah	ZEC		
Malachi	MAL		

What Time Is It?

Introduction

What time is it? From what I have learned from God's Word and been shown in visions and dreams, I believe that we are nearing the end of the world as prophesied in the Bible. It is very late. But there is more to the answer than that, though it is something that each person must decide for himself.

God has not left man completely in the dark about what will happen in the latter days. In His love and mercy He has given to us warnings through signs and prophecies. In the New Testament, MAT 24, we read how Jesus answered his disciples in plain, simple words and told them what signs they should look for. For example, in verses 7–8 we read: "For nation shall rise against nation, and kingdom against kingdom: and there shall be famines, and pestilences, and earthquakes, in divers places. All these are the beginning of sorrows." In verses 14–15 we read: "And this gospel of the kingdom shall be preached in all the world for a witness unto all nations; and then shall the end come. When ye therefore shall see the abomination of desolation, spoken of by Daniel the prophet, stand in the holy place, (whoso readeth, let him understand)"; in verse 21: "For then shall be great tribulation, such as was not since the beginning of the world to this time, no, nor ever shall be"; in verse 24: "For there shall arise false Christs, and false prophets, and shall shew great signs and wonders; insomuch that, if it were possible, they shall deceive the very elect"; and verse 29: "Immediately after the tribulation of those days shall the sun be darkened, and the moon shall not give her light, and the stars shall fall from heaven, and the powers of the heavens shall be shaken."

Although there are signs, Jesus informed us that only God knows the exact time of the end (MAT 24:36): "But of that day and hour knoweth no man, no, not the angels of heaven, but my Father only." And Jesus cautioned mankind (MAT 24:44), "Therefore be ye also ready: for in such an hour as ye think not the Son of man cometh." Mark also quoted Jesus in 13:33,37: "Take ye heed, watch and pray: for ye know not when the time is. . . . **And what I say unto you, I say unto all, Watch."** It is **TIME TO WATCH!** Are you watching? And **are you PREPARED?** Prophecies, one after another, are being fulfilled, and this is being written as a witness to inspire others to *watch and to be prepared* for the Lord's coming.

As this is being written, I wish it were possible to omit the pronoun "I." It is with deep humility and a feeling of unworthiness that I put on paper what God has shown me in these visions and dreams and how the Holy Spirit also gave the interpretations of the same. It is wonderful. I hope that you too will have this experience someday. If I have done wrong by being slow to write these experiences, I hope that God will forgive me. It was when I began to realize that I was denying the power of the Holy Spirit by keeping silent that I started to write, in the simplest of words, the wonderful things that God had shown me. If only I had seen scenes of joy and happiness, but there was nothing of the kind.

To read about this joy and happiness read MAT 25:34: "Then shall the King say unto them on his right hand, Come, ye blessed of my Father, inherit the kingdom prepared for you from the foundation of the world." Read also MAT 25:46: "And these shall go away into everlasting punishment: but the righteous into life eternal"; and REV 5:10: "And hast made us unto our God kings and priests: and we shall reign on the earth." REV 7:9 says: "After this I beheld, and, lo, a great multitude, which no man could number, of all nations, and kindreds, and people, and tongues, stood before the throne, and before the Lamb, clothed with white robes, and palms in their hands"; and also REV 7:16–17: "They shall hunger no more, neither thirst any more; neither shall the sun light on them, nor any heat. For the Lamb which is in the midst of the throne shall feed them, and shall lead them unto living fountains of waters: and God shall wipe away all tears from their eyes." If it were just possible that *all* men, *all* people, could be included in that number of joyous people, but it isn't possible, because of sin.

If not joy and happiness, then what are my visions and dreams all about? Judgments! Is God saying, "Woe, woe, woe," unto the inhabitants of the earth because of sin? There still is **TIME TO PREPARE. How much time we do not know,** but it seems to be running out. There still is *time for repentance,* time for a turning away from the sinful lusts of this life, the worldly desires, and a **time for turning to a more Christ-like life,** which alone can *lead to a life of joy and happiness in eternity.*

No doubt you too, when you were a child, had a few favorite Bible stories, taken from the Old Testament. I had several, one of which was taken from the first three chapters of the First Book of Samuel. In order to get the full impact of this story, please read these three chapters.

Oh, how Hannah prayed unto the Lord! He answered her prayers, and she bore a son and called his name Samuel. When he was still young, she gave him unto the Lord. She took him to the temple and left him with Eli, to serve the Lord. That this would happen when he was still a little child puzzled me. God did bless Hannah, though, and she had other children. As I grew older, these three chapters seemed to be full of lessons.

The part that especially interested me is in chapter 3, verses 13 and 15: "For I have told him [Eli] that I will judge his house for ever, for the iniquity which he knoweth: because his sons made themselves vile, and he restrained them not." And Samuel lay until the morning and opened the doors of the house of the Lord: And Samuel feared to shew Eli the vision."

Think about it. Samuel was just a child, but he had to give such a message to Eli, and Eli was a priest in the temple. God had already warned Eli, as you read in the previous chapter, I SAM 2:30–35, "For them that honour me I will honour, and they that despise me shall be lightly esteemed; . . . the days come, that I will cut off thine arm, and the arm of thy father's house, that there shall not be an old man in thine house . . . And thou shalt see an enemy in my habitation, in all the wealth which God shall give Israel: and there shall not be an old man in thine house for ever . . . And the man of thine, whom I shall not cut off from mine altar, shall be to consume thine eyes, and to grieve thine heart: and all the increase of thine house shall die in the flower of their age . . . And this shall be a sign unto thee, that shall come upon thy two sons, on Hophni and Phinehas; in one day they shall die both of them."

Thus judgment was to come upon him and his sons, because of their sins. Eli knew of his son's sins, and he must have just lightly spoken to them about it, because the message that was given to Samuel was: "His sons made themselves vile, *AND HE RESTRAINED THEM NOT.*" What happened?

In I SAM 4:17–18 we read: "And the messenger answered and said, Israel is fled before the Philistines, and there hath been also a great slaughter among the people, and thy two sons also, Hophni and Phinehas, are dead, and the ark of God is taken. And it came to pass, when he made mention of the ark of God, that he fell from off the seat backward by the side of the gate, and his neck brake, and he died: for he was an old man, and heavy. And he had judged Israel forty years." God had warned Eli. That which had been prophesied happened. What a lesson this is for parents.

How I loved to hear those words, "Samuel, Samuel," and the reply: "Speak, for thy servant heareth." How wonderful it was that the Lord would call and speak to a child. It wasn't until years later that I got the full message of this lesson. AMO 3:7 plainly states: "Surely the Lord GOD will do nothing, but he revealeth his secret unto his servants the prophets." Thus Eli had been warned, by God. Because he did not heed this warning, another one is given, through Samuel.

Isaiah, Jeremiah, Daniel, and Ezekiel, all prophesied of things that are to happen in the latter days. Things that were to take place during their lifetime were fulfilled. What a warning to mankind that what they prophesied about, things that were to happen *in the latter days, will also be fulfilled.* Thus the visions that you will read about will show forth some of God's warnings. He is a loving God and Father, but He is also a just God. The New Testament, therefore, adds to what had already been prophesied, and we would do well to heed these warnings. God has been very patient, giving the human race **time to repent and to accept Jesus Christ** as their personal Savior.

We too have a book of prophecy: Revelations. God has shown me in these visions and dreams and the interpretations of them that what was prophesied in the Book of Revelations about the latter days has begun, and we seem to be rapidly approaching the fulfillment of His prophecies.

The Big Question

Am I going to be like Eli and soft-pedal sin and the warnings and admonitions given us by God? Am I going to hold back the truth, as it was shown me, by the Holy Spirit, both in the visions and the interpretations of the same, because I fear what people will be thinking and saying about me? Or am I going to speak loud and clear about some of the practices of this day and time? Will I also be lukewarm, as we read in REV 3:15 and 16? "I know thy works, that thou art neither cold nor hot: I would thou wert cold or hot. So then because thou art lukewarm, and neither cold not hot, I will spue thee out of my mouth."

I shall endeavor, by the power of the Holy Spirit, to write it as it was, and is, revealed to me. *Why? Why?* EZE 3:18 says: "When I say unto the wicked, Thou shalt surely die; and thou givest him not warning, nor speakest to warn the wicked from his wicked way, to save his life; the same wicked man shall die in his iniquity; but his blood will I require at thine hand." What a judgment this was: *"BUT HIS BLOOD WILL I REQUIRE AT THINE HAND."*

Please also read EZE 33:1–11. Thanks be to God, praise and honor to His Holy Name, for we read in verse 11: "Say unto them, As I live, saith the Lord GOD, I have no pleasure in the death of the wicked; but that the wicked turn from his way and live: turn ye, turn ye from your evil ways; for why will ye die, O house of Israel?"

O Lord, I too plead for mercy and grace.
Speak Lord, Thy servant heareth.
May Thy Holy Spirit guide and direct me,
Bring to my remembrance Thy truths.
Take Thou my hands and lead me,
Thy will be done. Amen.

Not Left in the Dark

From Genesis to Revelation we can see how God warned one generation after another that if they did not turn *from their idolatrous, wicked ways,* certain judgments would be brought upon them. Wars, flood, droughts, severe windstorms, pestilence, hail, fire, earthquakes, and even captivity by an enemy were some of the judgments. Thus there were many warnings given to people of the past about the latter days. Similar warnings are given to us in this generation. They will also be given to future generations in order to warn people to be prepared for the coming of the Lord.

God even gave us a book of prophecy, the Book of Revelation. So many, many people would rather not read it. As I have often been told, "I have tried to read it, but don't understand it, so I would rather live each day as it comes. Why worry or study about the future?"

The very first chapter of Revelation, though, in verse 3, states: "Blessed is he that readeth, and they that hear the words of this prophecy, and keep those things which are written therein: for the time is at hand." What did the last part of that verse say? ***"FOR THE TIME IS AT HAND."*** Just think it over; that was almost two thousand years ago. So we are *that* much closer to the complete fulfillment of this prophecy.

Because the visions and dreams that I am going to write about point to these things that are to happen, as prophesied in the Book of Revelation, it would be wise to learn what Revelation is about. *Halley's Bible Handbook* provides an insight:

"The Revelation of Jesus Christ, which God gave unto him, to shew unto his servants things which must shortly come to pass; and he sent and signified it by his angel unto his servant John": Thus, in its first word, the book is avowedly predictive. That is what it was written for; to Unfold the Future, to Chart the Course and Destiny of the Church.

It is a very practical book. Even though it is a book of mystery, with many things we do not understand, it also has many things we do understand. Imbedded in its Mysterious Imagery are some of the most Salutary Warnings and most Precious Promises of all Scripture. Very likely John himself did not understand some of the Visions that were to be revealed only with the unfolding story of the passing ages. Nevertheless John's soul thrilled with exultation, as his mind dwelt on what he saw.

Alternating simplest truths with mystical symbolism, it is a book of undiluted optimism for God's people, assuring us again and again that we are under God's protection, with, come what may, a Life of Everlasting Blessedness ahead. And, alternating scenes between earth and heaven, it is also a book of the "Wrath of God," ever and anon contrasting the Joys of the Redeemed with the Agonies of the Lost. And, Oh, how we need to be reminded of that in this careless and godless generation."*

---

* *Halley's Bible Handbook,* p. 685. Copyright 1965. Used by permission.

A revelation of things to come. That is what the book calls itself, a *revealing, unveiling, explaining, making known,* of things to come (REV 1:1 and 1:3).

The first three chapters of Revelation are not difficult to understand. I hope that you will read them. It wasn't until the third vision that I saw or dreamt anything in connection with these chapters. The third vision was depicted in an easily understood portrayal. Thus the message to the Laodicean church, which Saint John was told to write, as he was writing the book, also applies to the churches in the latter days, the existing churches here on earth, when Jesus comes to judge the quick and the dead and to set up His Kingdom.

In JOE 2:28–32 and repeated in the New Testament (ACT 2:17–21), we read:

> And it shall come to pass afterward, that I will pour out my spirit upon all flesh; and your sons and your daughters shall prophesy, your old men shall dream dreams, your young men shall see visions: And also upon the servants and upon the handmaids in those days will I pour out my spirit. And I will shew wonders in the heavens and in the earth, blood, and fire, and pillars of smoke. The sun shall be turned into darkness, and the moon into blood, before the great and terrible day of the LORD come. And it shall come to pass, that whosoever shall call on the name of the LORD shall be delivered: for in Mount Zion and in Jerusalem shall be deliverance, as the LORD hath said, and in the remnant whom the LORD shall call.

Somehow it seems difficult for many people to accept these verses, as they look at me with questioning eyes or a shrug of the shoulder or say, "You and your dreams." But I will be denying the power of the Holy Spirit if I do not witness to what was shown and interpreted to me.

At the end of one dream, as I was about to wake up, I heard and saw in large letters: "AMOS 3:1–10." The text included, in verses 8–9: " . . . the Lord GOD hath spoken, who can but prophesy? Publish in the palaces at Ashdod, and in the palaces in the land of Egypt . . . " Reading these words I am compelled to publish the things that I have been shown.

A Necessary Warning

Before going any further, I need to tell you that in three of the visions I was shown a condition in the church. The first two visions showed me that because of my recognition of some of the things that were happening within the church I would be outside the organized church. The third vision was different. It showed me the general conditions in churches and God's displeasure about them.

With regard to being outside the church, we (my husband and I) would not turn our backs on the church. We know what God's word says in HEB 10:23–25: "Let us hold fast the profession of our faith without wavering; (for he is faithful that promised); And let us consider one another to provoke unto love and to good works: Not forsaking the assembling of ourselves together, as the manner of some is; but exhorting one another: and so much the more, as ye see the day approaching."

We were in a church service almost every Sunday. What I had to be convinced of was that the denomination that I was attending was not perfect either. I believe that this also was necessary so that what was being revealed to me was not to be told or written in the name of any particular denomination. It was not to draw attention to any single church or denomination. *But it should be a message to all who would read, listen, or hear the warnings that the last day is approaching. Repent, for the Kingdom of God is at hand.*

There are some things that I would rather not write about. But the truth must be told as it was revealed and interpreted to me. This is not unlike what happened to the prophets of old who spoke and wrote concerning the things that they had seen or were instructed to do. There were things that they did not understand, but they wrote about them as God directed them.

Trumpets

The dreams and visions that I saw seem to relate to the blowing of the trumpets in REV 8,9, and 10. REV 8:1–5 tells us:

> And when he had opened the seventh seal, there was silence in heaven about the space of half an hour. And I saw the seven angels which stood before God; and to them were given seven trumpets. And another angel came and stood at the altar, having a golden censer; and there was given unto him much incense, that he should offer it with the prayers of all saints upon the golden altar which was before the throne. And the smoke of the incense, which came with the prayers of the saints, ascended up before God out of the angel's hand. And the angel took the censer, and filled it with fire of the altar, and cast it into the earth: and there were voices, and thunderings, and lightnings, and an earthquake.

We will not see things that happen in heaven, but we will feel the results of the same, here on earth. *"The smoke of the incense, WHICH CAME WITH THE PRAYERS OF THE SAINTS, ASCENDED UP BEFORE GOD,"* yes, is the prayer of God's people, the true believers in Jesus Christ the Savior, asking for His guidance, protection, and a strengthening of faith. They realize that Satan is on a rampage, trying to deceive the elect, and because of the ungodly, terrible, sinful conditions throughout the world, conditions are worsening constantly. We see and hear about terrorism, wars, murders, rape, robberies, scandals, persecutions, all kinds of sexual sins, lying, cheating, *covetousness* (as had never been heard of before), disobedience in homes and schools, teachers fearing for their lives, and a general falling away from the churches. Lovers of pleasure more than lovers of God appear more and more prevalent. We are warned that there will be tribulations before the end. MAT 24:21–22 reads: "For then shall be great tribulation, such as was not since the beginning of the world to this time, no, nor ever shall be. And except those days should be shortened, there should no flesh be saved: but for the elect's sake those days shall be shortened."

God hears the cries and pleas of His children, and as he promised in His word, because of them the days would be shortened. *The angel fills the censer from the altar and casts it into the earth:* THE FIRE OF GOD'S WRATH. That which has been prophesied will happen during *the latter days.* And so there are *voices and thunderings and lightning and an earthquake.*

With power from on high, the Holy Spirit will come to the faithful few *that will dare to speak out* against the many sins committed throughout the world. Yes, these *voices* are reminders of the warnings *in God's word,* because of these ungodly, sinful conditions.

Let us consider one of these warnings. This is also from the Book of Revelations, chapter 21:8: "But the fearful, and unbelieving, and the abominable, and murderers, and whoremongers, and sorcerers, and idolaters, and all liars, shall have their part in the lake which burneth with fire and brimstone: which is the second death." *The second death!* Yes, this is eternal separation from God.

Thundering and lightning: God's powerful voice, representing his anger and chastening, with hailstones. ISA 30:30: "And the LORD shall cause his glorious voice to be heard, and shall shew the lighting down of his arm, with the indignation of his anger, and with the flame of a devouring fire, with scattering, and tempest, and hailstones. Then, *earthquake,* this is another form of judgment." In another chapter, where Isaiah mentions things that are to happen during the last days he says (chapter 2, verse 19): "And they shall go into the holes of the rocks, and into the caves of the earth, for fear of the LORD, and for the glory of his majesty, when he ariseth to shake terribly the earth."

It wasn't until May 1973 that I started to save newspaper clippings of things that were happening that had been prophesied to be happening during the latter days. Yes, calamities such as droughts, floods, earthquakes, ship disasters, fish kills, et cetera. Here is a report of an earthquake that I think we should especially notice. Why? Because it happened near Mount Ararat, where the Bible says the ark landed after the terrible flood. Remember what we read in the book of Genesis about that terrible flood during Noah's time? How all life on earth was lost except Noah and his family and the animals that were taken into the ark, at the Lord's command? What a terrible judgment had been brought upon the human race, the earth, because of sin.

Now the report of the earthquake which occurred November 25, 1976, in Ankara, Turkey: Tents, food, and medical supplies were rushed to Eastern Turkey, where officials estimate up to three thousand persons died in an earthquake that leveled about one hundred villages near Mount Ararat. A report three days later stated that 3,636 bodies had already been recovered and they feared the toll might reach five thousand. Official figures showed there were thirty thousand homeless and twelve thousand serious injuries, and the temperature had dipped to a low of five degrees. Since this earthquake happened near Mount Ararat, *couldn't this be a reminder, a voice from above?* Once before *judgment came upon the human race, because of their terrible transgressions.* In this case it was water, the great flood (GEN 7). The next will be a judgment by fire, as prophesied in many places in the Scriptures.

Quoting from a September 18, 1976, item in the *Birmingham Post Herald:* Two More Strong Earthquakes Send New Fears Rippling across Northern Italy.

> Udine, Italy—Strong tremors jolted the quake-ravaged Friuli area again Wednesday, knocking down hundreds of buildings and spreading new fears through the land THAT HAS BEEN SHAKING FOR MORE THAN FOUR MONTHS. Since May, 241 tremors have been recorded. Officials estimate that Wednesday's shocks had left 29,000 homeless, adding to the 70,000 already without shelter and living in tents since the disastrous May earthquakes.

Another terrible earthquake that took over fifteen thousand lives happened in Tabas, Iran, on September 18, 1978. It destroyed entire cities and villages in a farming region in Iran. Do we read or hear about such loss of life and destruction, destroyed water systems, so many homeless, and loss of food crops without thinking seriously, Who alone can cause them or let them happen? Isn't it God the Creator?

What a wonderful, different kind of earthquake we

read about in MAT 28:2: "And, behold, there was a great earthquake: for the angel of the Lord descended from heaven, and came and rolled back the stone from the door, and sat upon it." In MAT 27:51 we read that when Jesus died ". . . the veil of the temple was rent in twain from the top to the bottom; and the earth did quake, and the rocks rent." Thus only God the Creator can permit or cause an earthquake. Some people say, "There have always been thunderstorms, hailstorms, and earthquakes." Yes, there have, *and there will be more.* God is speaking, warning, each time that it happens, as we read in Ezekiel, time and time again (fifty-one places): "*THEY SHALL KNOW THAT I AM THE LORD.*" Warnings, warnings, but man takes them so lightly. *Yes, God controls nature.*

Didn't God give Noah instructions to build the ark? Didn't he tell him what would happen? GEN 6:5 tell us: "And GOD saw that the wickedness of man was great in the earth, and that every imagination of the thoughts of his heart was only evil continually." Continuing with verse 8: "But Noah found grace in the eyes of the LORD," and verses 12–13: "And God looked upon the earth, and, behold, it was corrupt; for all flesh had corrupted his way upon the earth. And God said unto Noah, The end of all flesh is come before me; for the earth is filled with violence through them; and, behold, I will destroy them with the earth."

Didn't the people, most likely, make fun of Noah as he was building the ark? Did they listen to him? No! Then suddenly the doors of the ark were closed and it began to rain, and rain it did. Only too late did they realize that what had been told them had now started, and all except Noah and his family were lost.

Do we need another proof? AMO 4:6–7: "And I also have given you cleanness of teeth in all your cities, and want of bread in all your places: yet have ye not returned unto me, saith the LORD. And also I have withholden the rain from you, when there were yet three months to the harvest: and I caused it to rain upon one city, and caused it not to rain upon another city: one piece was rained upon, and the piece whereupon it rained not withered." Didn't Isaiah, Jeremiah, Ezekiel, and Daniel warn Israel time and time again, telling them what God had revealed unto them, such as the wars and that they would be taken captive, all because they had transgressed against the Lord? Didn't God use individuals to bring His message and warnings to the people? *Yes. Give them time to repent? But did they listen? Suddenly it was too late.* No doubt they too thought how terrible were some of the things that did happen. In GAL 6:7–8 we read: "Be not deceived; God is not mocked: for whatsoever a man soweth, that shall he also reap. For he that soweth to his flesh shall of the flesh reap corruption; but he that soweth to the Spirit shall of the Spirit reap life everlasting."

After the angel threw the fire from the altar to the earth, we read in REV 8:6, "and the seven angels which had the seven trumpets prepared themselves to sound." Will we hear them, here on earth? No, they sound in heaven, but the results of their sounding will be felt on earth (verse 7): "The first angel sounded, and there followed hail and fire mingled with blood, and they were cast upon the earth: and the third part of trees was burnt up, and all green grass was burnt up." The prophets speak of hail as a means of punishing the wicked. ISA 28:2: "Behold, the Lord hath a mighty and strong one, which as a tempest of hail and a destroying storm, as a flood of mighty waters overflowing, shall cast down to the earth with the hand." And also EZE 38:22: "And I will plead against him with pestilence and with blood; and I will rain upon him, and upon his bands, and upon the many people that are with him, an overflowing rain, and great hailstones, fire, and brimstone." Hail would be something that hurts, crushes, and is damaging to man and crops.

Fire, the very fire of God's wrath, *WITH THE HEAT OF THE SUN AND NO REFRESHING RAIN TO COOL, WHICH MINGLED WITH BLOOD, MEANT IT WOULD BRING DEATH TO MANY, MANY PEOPLE, DROUGHTS, YES, DROUGHTS.* And so we shall now consider the blowing of the first trumpet, as it was revealed to me in the first vision.

The First Trumpet

It was May 1965. It had been a very busy day. Vacation Bible School was just two weeks away, and knowing that there would be very little time, during those two weeks, for doing certain things about the house, I had worked very hard and was really tired. I was to be in full charge of Vacation Bible School that year because we were going through a vacancy. A new pastor had not yet been called.

It was 10:15 P.M. The alarm would soon be ringing, and my husband would be coming out for that cup of coffee before he started off to work. He was working the eleven-to-seven shift for the L&N railroad. There went the alarm. Yes, it wouldn't be long now before I'd be hopping into bed, and soon I'd be sound asleep. These were my thoughts. As a rule I slept soundly, *but* this night was to be an exception.

N-O-W

I don't know what time it was when I had this first vivid dream or vision. As I was walking along a pathway, I came to an outhouse. I went in. The walls had cracks between the boards. Look, there was a man's hand coming through one of the cracks. He was dressed in a black robe. I pulled back so that he could not reach me. Some people were coming up the path, and they just swept him along with them. Then I saw my husband coming; what a relief. I joined him, and together we walked a short distance and entered into the sanctuary. The next thing I knew we were walking out, hand in hand, and I had such a calm feeling, until I heard a voice from the choir loft: "I'll get you yet." There was that same man again, but the people just took him by the shoulders and turned him. Thus I was so disturbed and trembling, and together my husband and I went out the gate. When we were on the sidewalk, there were people coming from every direction, Huntington Avenue, Althea Street, Comfort Street, and Union Avenue. Oh, how happy they all seemed to be. All their faces had such a happy, peaceful expression. It was so different from what I had just experienced.

As we walked toward the corner, Henry, my husband, said, "Shall we walk home or ride up the hill?"

I answered, "It is already the eleventh hour; let's ride up."

Whenever I think about it now, it seems so strange that I would say something like that, because people do not come from church services at the eleventh hour, at night. We walked to the corner to wait for the vehicle that was to take us home. The streetcar or bus, I know not which, stopped in the middle of the block. Suddenly the sky to the right front of us became very bright and oh, so beautiful. Look; picture it with me. The pretty bright clouds and a large head appeared, in all that beauty, *but* its cheeks were puffed out, as if in anger, and it blew out of its mouth, in huge letters, stretching across the sky: "N-O-W." Yes, it was the word "NOW."

Trembling, I said to may husband, "Did you see that?"

He answered, "Sh, sh, folks will think you are crazy."

Because I had been talking to him, I missed what was happening in the sky just to the right of me. When I did see it, there was only a "2" and "19" left; the other had faded. Straining, I tried to make out what it could have been. While I was doing that, just to the right of where the letters and numbers had been, out of the sky, an animal's head, like a calf's head, appeared. It bent down to the ground and with its breath seemed to consume every green thing in sight, and nothing but brown stubble was left.

Suddenly I was awake. Where was I? Looking about, I finally realized that I was in my own bedroom. What was all this? That head angrily, with cheeks puffed out, blowing those huge letters: "N-O-W," clear across the sky? I just could not go back to sleep. That "2" and "19"? Yes, it was only two weeks now before Vacation Bible School would start. "Nineteen," no, that was not the date. No, it had nothing to do with Vacation Bible School, because there was that great big "N-O-W," yes, and the calf's head.

As I was lying there, thinking, it slowly seemed to unfold, step by step, and I am sure that it was by the power of the Holy Spirit that I began to understand what I had been shown in the vision.

Symbols and Their Meanings
1. Seeking relief: Getting away from disturbances.
2. Cracks between the boards: My concern and heaviness of heart are visible to others.

3. Man in the black robe: The ministry.
4. Hand through the cracks: They would like to silence me.
5. People just sweep him along: Other people also realize the condition in some of the churches.
6. Husband comes: For some time already he has been bringing to my attention some of the things that are happening in some of the churches.
7. We enter the sanctuary: His admonition always is: "The Bible says."
8. Peaceful feeling: Only God's word can quiet the disturbed heart.
9. I'll get you yet: The ministry again.
10. People turn him about: The laity speak also.
11. Going out the gate: Leaving the church to which I belonged.
12. Happy people: Christians, also from other denominations, on the way to their heavenly home.
13. Walk or ride up: Walking would mean we were *trying* to go by our own righteousness, going by conveyance, going God's way, saved by grace.
14. Eleventh hour: Very late. Time is growing short.
15. Bright, beautiful opening in the sky: The beauty of the heavenly.
16. Large head: The Lion of the Tribe of Judah, the Lamb of God, the Word of God.
17. Cheeks puffed out blowing: Anger because of sin.
18. "N-O-W": The trumpets will begin to blow as prophesied in the Book of Revelation.
19. "2"—"19": Another vision followed during February 19 ? ?
20. Calf's head: One of the four beasts serving and praising God.
21. Breath: Of God's anger, because man's iniquities, all

his transgressions, are known to Him.
22. Consumes every green thing: Droughts.

Now let us put it all together and get the full meaning and lesson of this vision. So I had *gone into an outhouse.* From time to time there were things happening in the church that really disturbed me. One had happened that seemed almost unbelievable, because it hindered the work of the church and God's will to "Go ye therefore."

I had gone to an executive board meeting in Indiana. Several different kinds of materials that could help to promote the work of our missionary societies were shown to us and explained. One of these was a play, *Mary and Martha Become Missionaries.* After reading it over twice, I was convinced that the lesson it taught was exactly what our society needed. Since all material used in our missionary societies had to be approved by the pastor, after my return home I gave it to him for his approval, with the hope that he would return it shortly, so that we could learn, rehearse, and present it some evening before the real cold weather.

Four weeks passed, and he had not returned it. When I questioned him, he said that he had mailed it. "Yes, it was okay," he added. Mailed it? I sent for another copy, and soon my missionary society was at work rehearsing our parts.

All agreed that what this play was trying to teach us was exactly what we should be doing, *but we were not.* We were not calling on visitors that had attended church services, the unchurched, sick, aged, needy, and widows. The last act called for the pastor to commend the women for what they had been doing. Since I thought and felt sure that this would give our pastor a wonderful opportunity to encourage all our members to become more active, more mission-minded, and the play called for the pastor to do so, I asked our pastor to take this part. His answer was: "No, Mrs. Miller, I would rather not. Why not have a woman dress as a man and play the pastor's part?" This was more than I could take. I told him in strong words that this play showed us what we should be doing but were not. It was serious business and I was just not going to have folks laughing at some woman dressed as a man and spoil the whole thoughts and lesson of the play. (*This was before so many women wore pants.*) Since he would not take the part, I would, as District President. For years and years we had been praying *that Thy word may not be bound but have free course and be preached to the joy and edifying of Christ's holy people.* But what had happened? For over fifty years God's word had been bound to that little church on the corner, the only one of its denomination in a large and growing city.

When we met for rehearsals we prayed, at my request. We changed the name of the play to *Prayer Changes Things.* And did it? Yes, *and how!* We asked the church council for permission to organize another church in an area where many of the older people lived. Many did not have cars and had to transfer to a second streetcar in order to get to church. At first we were refused. *And how!* Finally, they consented. Less than a year later, we were a self-supporting congregation, on the other side of town. We had told them that God was able to bless two congregations in this growing city, and oh, how God did prove it to everyone when, three years later, the first church dedicated their new, beautiful sanctuary. Never did the pastor or the church council admit that they had been wrong or say that they were sorry for all that had been said and done.

There were many other things that happened at that

first church before we left, but I shall only write about one more. This happened when I visited a woman that was to have surgery. She was so frightened. What would happen, yes, become of her children? Because the doctors thought that she had cancer, they told her that only an operation could prolong her life. She was a widow. I made a special trip to the pastor's home, by streetcar, to explain the situation to him. I asked him to visit her—she definitely needed spiritual guidance—but I was told that she was of a different faith. But she hadn't been to any church in years, she had told me and also the pastor. Although I had gone out of my way to make this request, he gave me no satisfaction. All I could say was: "Well, you may let her down, *but I will not.*" He did go, though, and she was baptized and her family joined the church also.

It wasn't long before a third church, a mission, was started on the side of town where we lived. It seemed to happen, time and again, at Ladies Aid meetings, that when some matter was being discussed or some questions asked about the topic being studied, the pastor, who always was present, would give some long explanation or answer of some kind, and I suppose his words they thought should be final. I was bold enough to speak up and, with a Bible passage or two, give an answer that was much more to the point and understandable. Isn't it God's word that should instruct us? I still remember the questioning look the minister's wife would give him when I did this, but isn't it God's words that should guide and direct us? Thus the man in the vision is the ministry. It was also he that said, "I'll get you yet."

There was a fence around the property of the church that I attended until I married at the age of twenty-four. In the vision, the gate was open, and so we went out and met all those happy people, coming from all directions. Yes, no doubt, people from other denominations. *People that also were on their way home:* all believers in our Lord and Savior Jesus Christ are now, at the eleventh hour, looking forward to an eternal home with Him.

Shall we walk or ride up the hill? Our home was on the other side of the hill. Well, if we walked home, wouldn't that mean that we were depending on our own righteousness? *Riding up the hill* that we were depending on the Holy Spirit to guide and direct us to our heavenly home? Yes, I believe so. *The conveyance stopped in the middle of the block;* that meant that our time had not yet come. *The eleventh hour,* according to what I saw later, was an admittance that I believe the time is growing short. Yes, it is very late.

Some of the things that would happen, during the latter days, that had been prophesied many, many years ago were now gradually going to take place. Oh, yes, sure, many prophecies have already been fulfilled, but *now* those telling of the things that will take place during the latter days are beginning to be fulfilled more, and more rapidly.

Just picture, if you will, in the darkness of the night a huge spot in the sky becoming so bright and beautiful. But there from the center of it appears a large head, with cheeks puffed out, angrily blowing those huge letters: "N-O-W," out across the sky. Words just cannot describe how I felt when it happened. There will be more about this later.

I asked my husband if he had seen it, and he answered, "SH, sh, folks will think you're crazy provides a good picture of how some people accept the message. One said, "You and your dreams." Some just shrug their shoulders or give me a doubtful look. So few people want to accept it, that there will be dreams and visions, and that it was already prophesied in Old Testament times (JOE 2:28–30, see page O) and repeated in the New Testament (ACT 2), where we read (verses 16–21).

> But this is that which was spoken by the prophet Joel; And it shall come to pass in the last days, saith God, I will pour out of my Spirit upon all flesh: and your sons and your daughters shall prophesy, and your young men shall see visions, and your old men shall dream dreams: And on my servants and on my handmaidens I will pour out in those days of my Spirit; and they shall prophesy: And I will shew wonders in heaven above, and signs in the earth beneath: blood, and fire, and vapour of smoke: The sun shall be turned into darkness, and the moon into blood, before the great and notable day of the Lord come: And it shall come to pass, that *whosoever shall call on the name of the Lord shall be saved.*

There will be dreams and visions in the last days. Somebody, somewhere, will be having them, and it is denying the power of the Holy Spirit to deny this or to make light of the same. God, in His love and mercy, has told us in many places, in His Holy Word, that we could tell when the time was approaching by certain things that would be taking place about us. *Are you watching? What time is it?*

Now the "2" and "19," what could they have been? It wasn't until 1973, when I was filing a write-up of a vision, that I noticed a previously filed paper dated February 1969. Quickly I took it out and read it. Yes, there it was, on February, 19—the "2" and the "19." The second trumpet had sounded, had been revealed to me, but I had been so busy that I didn't realize the importance of what had been shown me. More will be said about this later.

And what did the animal's head, like a calf's head *that*

was with its breath destroying every green thing, along the ground, until there was only brown stubble left mean? DROUGHTS, yes, there will be a period of droughts. I started keeping newspaper clippings in 1973, but I wish that I had started sooner. Have there been droughts? I shall only write up a few reports about some of them.

From a newspaper clipping, June 23, 1973: "Over more than three years Mauritania, and five other countries in Africa, have suffered from severe drought. Millions of cattle, goats, and sheep have died of thirst and hunger." Just think of the hardship that caused for the people of the area.

In January 6, 1974, drought hit the economy of Africa hard. Man, land, and beast suffered in a pitiless dry spell for months and, in some places, *up to five years* without rain. Across Africa the human toll was enormous. Tens of thousands of people were dead, hundreds of thousands starving, millions undernourished and feeble. West Africa's worst drought in *half a century* dried up lakes, rivers, and wells in the parched famine zones.

In July 1974 I saw a headline: "Midlands Drought Called Worst since 1930 As Crops and Cattle Die." In July 1975, I saw a picture in a newspaper with the caption: "Skull and skeleton of a cow, near a stream, where it died from drinking sea water in wake of a catastrophic drought in the African nation of Senegal."

In March 1973 water was rationed in St. Lucia because of droughts. In July 25, 1975, droughts hit western beef producers. In November 21, 1976, the South Dakota drought brought pleas for help.

Droughts and famines continue. Now it is October 1976. What about the terrible droughts in Britain and Western Europe? Remember how water had to be rationed in California? There had been so little snow on the mountains and oh, so little rain. In the summer of 1977 a drought hit the southeastern states. Just think of all the countries that had to buy grain from the United States during the past years. Is it necessary to list any further evidence? All this and more has happened since the calf's head appeared, *bending down from the sky and destroying, with its breath, every green thing in sight, until there was nothing but brown stubble* . . . a judgment, the fire of God's wrath.

Now let us relate what has been written about the vision with the blowing of the first trumpet in REV 8:7: Droughts! I did not see hail and fire mingled with blood, *true,* but when the first trumpet sounded and hail and fire, mingled with blood, were cast upon the earth, it meant that *a judgment from God was to come upon the earth and it would cause droughts.*

Consider the large head in my vision that blew the word "N-O-W" into the sky. Bear in mind that much of what is written in the Book of Revelation is *FIGURATIVE* or *SYMBOLIC* and also that what was shown me is also symbolic. So whose head was it? Remember, the sky became so bright and beautiful and out of this beauty the head appeared.

In REV 4:1 we read: "After this I looked, and, behold, a door was opened in heaven: and the first voice which I heard was as it were of a trumpet talking with me; which said, Come up hither, and I will shew thee things which must be hereafter." I too saw the clouds open, and I was shown things that will happen hereafter. The next four verses, 2–5, are easy to understand. God is sitting on a throne; the rainbow is his covenant with man; He will not destroy the earth again with a flood. Then there are the twenty-four elders, who are the heads of the twelve tribes of Israel and the twelve apostles. There is lightning and thundering and voices, yes, warnings, and the seven lamps of fire, burning before the throne, are the seven spirits of God.

Now, verses 6–8 read: "And before the throne there was a sea of glass like unto crystal: and in the midst of the throne, and round about the throne, were four beasts full of eyes before and behind. And the first beast was like a lion, and the second beast like a calf, and the third beast had a face as a man, and the fourth beast was like a flying eagle. And the four beasts had each of them six wings about him; and they were full of eyes within: and they rest not day and night, saying, Holy, holy, holy, Lord God Almighty, which was, and is, and is to come." Continuing with verse 11: "Thou art worthy, O Lord, to receive glory and honour and power: for thou hast created all things, and for thy pleasure they are and were created." But what has man become, and what has he done to the things that God created? The beasts, being full of eyes, had beheld the wickedness of man.

And so the scene is set. Chapter 5, verses 1–7, reads:

> And I saw in the right hand of him that sat on the throne a book written within and on the backside, sealed with seven seals. And I saw a strong angel proclaiming with a loud voice, Who is worthy to open the book, and to loose the seals thereof? And no man in heaven, nor in earth, neither under the earth, was able to open the book, neither to look thereon. And I wept much, because no man was found worthy to open and to read the book, neither to look thereon. And one of the elders saith unto me, Weep not: behold, the Lion of the tribe of Judah, the Root of David, hath prevailed to open the book, and to loose the seven seals thereof. And I beheld, and, lo, in the midst of the throne and of the four beasts, and in the midst of the elders, stood a Lamb as it had been slain, having seven

horns and seven eyes, which are the seven Spirits of God sent forth into all the earth. And he came and took the book out of the right hand of him that sat upon the throne.

He was called *the Lion of the Tribe of Judah.* This title belongs only to Jesus, and so that we may be sure, and that there can be no doubt, we read in verse 6: "STOOD A LAMB, AS IT HAD BEEN SLAIN," et cetera. *And so it was HE that took the book and only HE that was worthy to open the seals that would foretell what was about to happen,* as we read in REV 4:1: "And I will show thee things which must be hereafter." Jesus, the Son of God, the Lamb of God that taketh away the sins of the world, *but also the Word,* as we read in JOH 1:1–3: "In the beginning was the Word, and the Word was with God, and the Word was God. The same was in the beginning with God. All things were made by him; and without him was not any thing made that was made."

Thus *the Lion of the Tribe of Judah that had become the Lamb of God that taketh away the sins of the world and also the Word was the only one that could give the command "N-O-W," yes, now.* That which was prophesied would happen during the last days was about to begin.

Let us consider *the sounding of the trumpets.* AMO 3:8: "The lion hath roared, who will not fear: the Lord God hath spoken, who can but prophesy?" The people of early times were familiar with and no doubt knew and had heard many times how God sent hail and fire down upon Egypt. Finally, there was also the shedding of blood, when all the firstborn died in one night. What a shedding, a loss of blood! They found out, too late, that the wrath of God had come down upon them, because they would not let God's people go. Judgments! First, let us look at *hail.* EXO 9:18: "Behold, tomorrow about this time I will cause it to rain a very grievous hail, such as hath not been in Egypt since the foundation thereof even until now." Yes, and it happened. EXO 9:24: "So there was hail, and fire mingled with the hail, very grievous, such as there was none like it in all the land of Egypt since it became a nation." So there was fire mingled with hail. ISA 28:17 tells us: "Judgment also will I lay to the line, and righteousness to the plummet: and the hail shall sweep away the refuge of lies, and the waters shall overflow the hiding place." Fire was also present when hail fell upon Egypt. Thus hail is a judgment brought on by the *fire* of God's wrath, because of sin. PSA 18:7–8, 12–13: "Then the earth shook and trembled; the foundations also of the hills moved and were shaken, because he was wroth. There went up a smoke out of his nostrils, and fire out of his mouth devoured: coals were kindled by it . . . At the brightness that was before him his thick clouds passed, hail stones and coals of fire. The LORD also thundered in the heavens, and the Highest gave his voice; hail stones and coals of fire." JER 21:13: "O house of David, thus saith the LORD; Execute judgment in the morning, and deliver him that is spoiled out of the hand of the oppressor, lest my fury go out like fire, and burn that none can quench it, because of the evil of your doings."

EZE 22:20, "As they gather silver, and brass, and iron, and lead, and tin, into the midst of the furnace, to blow the fire upon it, to melt it; so will I gather you in mine anger and in my fury, and I will leave you there, and melt you." With one of God's first creations, with the heat of the sun, and with the withholding of the rain the fire of His wrath can cause such terrible *droughts.* And hail and fire were mingled with blood.

Thus far I have quoted only Old Testament Scripture passages. Here is one from the New Testament. Yes, it will happen in the latter days. 2TH 1:7–8: "And to you who are troubled rest with us, when the Lord Jesus shall be revealed from heaven with his mighty angels, In flaming fire taking vengeance on them that know not God, and that obey not the gospel of our Lord Jesus Christ." Only the blood of Jesus Christ, our Savior, can cleanse us from all sin. But so many reject this saving grace and mercy. 1JO 1:7: "But if we walk in the light, as he is in the light, we have fellowship one with another, and the blood of Jesus Christ his Son cleanseth us from all sin." Thus *blood mingled with hail and fire* is to remind man that his rejection of God's love, grace, and mercy, his refusal to be cleansed by the blood of Jesus Christ, the Savior, is bringing upon man the judgments that you have been reading about.

The calf that we read about in REV 4:7–8, the second beast that was mentioned, *being full of eyes,* rested not day or night, saying, "Holy, holy, holy, Lord God Almighty, which was and is and is to come," and announced with its breath, carrying out what had been prophesied many years ago (REV 8:7): " . . . and the third part of trees was burnt up, and all green grass was burnt up." The very same *judgment,* hail, fire, mingled with blood. *Droughts,* et cetera, are continuing. It appears that NOW the *first trumpet* has sounded.

The Second Trumpet

This second vision was typed up and put away into the file without much thought being given to it. Why? In the first place, I wasn't giving much thought to the Book of Revelation at the time, and second I was so deeply concerned with temporal matters.

It was at this time that the interstate highway plans were being accelerated. Surveyors were behind the house almost daily. We were going north, south, east, and west, looking for another place to live where we could garden. Since my husband was retired, gardening would help financially, in addition to being a hobby. Then the appraiser came. We learned that about 160 feet, including a corner of the garage, was what they were planning to take. The garden area would be gone, plus all the fruit trees, grapevines, and strawberry and blueberry bushes. How wonderfully, though, God did lead and direct us through those days. Soon after they settled with us financially, there was an ad in the daily paper: "House For Sale, by owner, in Wilsonville." What a surprise it was when we first saw the house! There was a nice brick house in the center of a two-acre knoll. Little had I hoped or expected ever to have one like it. So often when we went riding through the country on a Sunday afternoon we would see such places and comment, "How pretty." We both almost immediately realized that this was the kind of place we had been seeking. Here was a home in a small town where we could garden and also be away from the noise and traffic of the city.

This home in the country apparently was God's plan. We were to be almost alone . . . just daily living with *Him,* with more time to meditate on His word, His *love,* and His mercy . . . *yes,* and His guidance. We were to have a closer walk with Him. I was to be away from all the activities that I had taken a part in, both in the church and the community. Experience has taught me *that we can be too busy being busy.* Often I have thought about Moses, how he had to leave and live for forty years away from all the activities that he had grown up in and experienced.

The Saturday before we moved, a strange thing happened. At 9:15 P.M. I received a call asking me to play for the service at a small church in the neighborhood. I had attended services there only once in the twelve years that we lived in the area. I decided to play for them, even though it meant playing a piano instead of an organ, and I also wanted to attend their adult Bible Class. The lesson was GAL 1:15–19: "But when it pleased God, who separated me from my mother's womb, and called me by his grace," Saint Paul wrote (verse 16): "To reveal his Son in me, that I might preach him among the heathen; immediately I conferred not with flesh and blood: Neither went I up to Jerusalem to them which were apostles before me; but I went into Arabia, and returned again unto Damascus. Then after three years I went up to Jerusalem to see Peter, and abode with him fifteen days. But other of the apostles saw I none, save James the Lord's brother."

I sat there, listening intently, as they read and discussed the above. Then they mentioned how Moses was drawn aside before God called him to lead the children of Israel out of Egypt. Then they discussed how Jesus drew aside for forty days into the wilderness before He started his ministry. By now I realized that this lesson was for me. God sure does work in mysterious ways His wonders to perform. I was deep in thought when I suddenly heard the teacher say, "Mrs. Miller, maybe you would like to add a few words to the lesson of today. We still have seven minutes." She was a substitute teacher for that day. Now what? There was just one thing to do, tell them the truth. I told them that we were moving the following Wednesday and that I too would be forty miles away from all the activities that I had taken part in. I do not drive, so I would not be going back and forth. Yes, this lesson was for me. I would just bow to the Lord's will and say, *"Thy will be done."* They too were amazed at what had happened that morning. This was in 1970. I had already had the first two visions, but then in 1973 there was the all-important one, as you will see later.

Thus, as mentioned earlier in this chapter, we were so busy looking for a new homesite that this vision was typed up and filed. While filing the write-up of the third vision and thinking, *Truly this is a vision of the sounding of the third trumpet,* I came across the account of the second trumpet in the file. Now everything became more and more interesting and important. I was sure that what was happening was from God.

A MESSENGER

Now the second vision and its interpretation: Entering the basement of a church building, I saw a room full of children. Some were restless, others noisy, and others unruly. As I looked about the room and saw it all, I was tempted to call them to order . . . to quiet them. But *no,* I could not do that now. I could do so only when in charge of a Sunday school or Vacation Bible School. *But I am no longer in charge; others have taken over. Where are they?*

I left, going up the stairs and out the door. There, seated on the lawn in front of the church, were all the grown-ups, dressed in their best, listening intently to a speaker. Why weren't they, or a few of them, with the children? That was my thought. Without a word, I proceeded out through the gate, and with one last look at all their finery and faces I went on my way, towards home, across Huntington Avenue, then following along on Union Avenue, which led across a railroad bridge. Only four more blocks and I would be starting up the hill, then down on the other side, which would lead to home. As I was about one-fourth of the way across the bridge, *a man suddenly appeared.* He said, "I would advise you to keep right on going. We have had a terrible landslide just behind you, and the heavy mud and water are rapidly coming this way." Even as he spoke, I looked, and all that I could see was huge waves of mud. *But I had just come from there.* I thanked the man and hurried on my way, *but the bridge was already gone* and I had to step from rock to rock, yes, from one rock to another. How strange, though, some looked so shaky, even uneven, but each time that I stepped on one it felt so safe. Now I came to one that looked especially difficult, but as I stepped on it there was the strongest foothold, and so I could safely go ahead. From then on they seemed even firmer, and I could travel on faster. It wasn't long before I was on the other side, safe, on level ground. Now to the right of me was a huge flat rock, and the whole area around it was beautifully landscaped. I woke up suddenly and realized that I was in my own room.

How strange! The interpretation of this vision also shows *lukewarm conditions in some of the churches.* This time it brought the children to my attention, some of them restless. Thus the first questions: Why are these children alone? First, the interpretation seems to say that they are children of God. They were not in the sanctuary, but in the basement. It was not their spiritual needs that were being neglected entirely. They needed guidance, love, and care in other ways, also, *just as the members of a congregation do.* We are all called the children of God. How many of the "children," the church members, ever see the pastor, the shepherd of the flock, except on Sundays and in some churches on Wednesday nights? Conventions, conferences, retreats, association meetings, et cetera, take so much of the pastor's time. And the members? They are at the church almost all day on Sunday, then attending again on Wednesday night. There are also choir rehearsals, teachers' meetings, mission society meetings, and others, *yes, always learning,* as one might say, *so that there is so little time to put to practice some of what they have learned.* Little time is given to those having problems of one sort or another . . . little time for those words of kindness, encouragement, love, or a helping hand. These are the people that were outside, sitting on the lawn, listening intently to a speaker.

We can even go further. There were also parents that were looking after their own interests. They were dressed in their best, because of their covetous ways, when so many mothers were working not because they need the money, but so that they could have so many of the extras of this day and time. Many children are left to themselves or are put in nursery schools or kindergartens. Yes, even babies have someone else to take care of them while the mothers work. Other people are laying the foundation for the children's lives because the mothers are at work. Coming home tired and still having to take care of the responsibilities of the home, the parents give the children so little love and attention. Is this the way that God planned the family, the home? We often find children in the nursery during church services that should be in the service, because the parents think of their own comfort and not about the foundation that should be laid for a good Christian life for the child.

And so I left; I started for home. *A man suddenly appeared.* Yes, I believe that he was a messenger from God. I was advised to keep right on going because of a terrible landslide. The landslide was coming rapidly. I saw it, *but I had just come from there. Now all was covered with mud.* What I saw was huge waves of mud, and they were rapidly coming toward me. What I had been told was that "there has been a terrible landslide." Now the Book of Revelation says (8:8): " . . . and as it were a great mountain burning with fire was cast into the sea . . . " A *fiery* mountain cast into the sea would cause *lava.* I saw mud. Here we have the figurative language of the Book of Revelation again. God's anger has increased and now looms up like a mountain and is cast into the sea, causing more hardships for the human race because of their unbelief and sin. Just as the plagues came upon Egypt, one after another, so the judgments of God are also now coming upon the human race, as it was prophesied that they would. Remember REV 8:8–9.

So what has happened? Remember the sliding hill in Abervan? Waves of mud hit a school. One hundred and sixteen children died. "The people will never recover from this terrible shock" is what we recently read again in the papers. They also stated that the 116 graves were all together. It was also told on TV that twelve thousand dollars had been given to each family that had lost a child in this terrible catastrophe.

Do you remember this headline: "Lava Threatens to Close Harbor Reykjavik?" A stream of glowing lava 220 yards wide threatened to close the harbor of deserted Reimer Island, authorities reported Tuesday, February 7, 1973. Continuing: "In the background the mighty Helgafjell volcano continued its eruption for the 16th day. The authorities said the lava stream was only 28 yards from the harbor entrance at 10:00 C.S.T., Tuesday. It travels at a speed of about 8 yards an hour. Rescue officials said they could do nothing to halt the lava stream, and 300 policemen, firemen and civil workers in the island waited idly for the lava to close the harbor, ONCE ICELAND'S LEADING FISHING PORT."

Have the creatures in the sea been affected in any way? Yes, they have. Several years ago (after the vision), when I went to Rhode Island to visit my people, there were no clams or lobsters. How I missed them! They were something I always looked forward to when making that trip up north.

My next trip was to St. Petersburg, Florida. They were having a *RED TIDE.* Remember when no oysters or shrimp were available from the gulf, none to be sold? Remember when Portugal for a whole year had to discontinue its sardine fishing? Remember how we heard, just recently, that the James River was contaminated with Kepone and no fishing was allowed? Some of it still is contaminated. Haven't you read that there could be no commercial fishing in the Coosa River in Alabama? Someone may say, "WELL, THAT WAS CAUSED BY MAN." Doesn't God let the foolishness of men often bring him into trouble? Man had nothing to do with that terrible landslide that killed 116 children, nor did he have anything to do with the lava flow that closed the harbor in Iceland that had once been its leading fishing port. As you will see, conditions are getting worse as time goes on. So many red tides, et cetera. *Are you watching?*

The April 1, 1973, edition of *National Geographic* states (p. 483): In the Summer of 1972 lobster prices fell to $1.00 a pound because of a RED TIDE. The organism that causes this phenomenon poisons clams, though it does not affect lobsters. Newspaper headlines spoke of "Shellfish," but housewives and diners refused to touch lobsters until the scare had passed. I would do likewise.

On November 3, by Fort Myers, Florida, an outbreak of *red tide* and northerly winds combined to pile *thousands of dead fish onto the gulf coast beaches,* from Sanibel Island to Charlotte Harbor, bringing in large numbers of sharks to feed on the rotting fish.

"Marine life contaminated," South Vietnam said. Japan's Social and Health Ministry disclosed in Yokohama that it has impounded *twenty-four tons of frozen shrimp from South Vietnam,* pending the outcome of tests. A finding by Japan that the shrimp were unfit for human consumption would virtually rule out foreign markets *for shrimp, crabs, and fish.* If there is any question about these, should man eat them? Would you?

In Miami, Florida, a biologist, who found the source of a *"whirling death"* fish disease that forced health officials to close part of Florida's Biscayne Bay, said that the toxin offered little danger to humans (?). Do you want to eat something like that? The biologist speculated that about the only way a human could get the disease would be to eat the stomach, or viscera, of affected fish, and those are the organs that are thrown away when fish are cleaned. Yes, but what the fish eat determines whether they live or grow or die. *Is the love of money causing such things to be sold on the market?* The end of this article reads: "The fishing and swimming ban was imposed after THOUSANDS OF FISH were seen twirling madly before popping up dead on the surface."

On February 3, 1977, four pilot whales were found dead on the shores of Fort George Inlet early one Monday. Rescue workers had managed to refloat the beached whales the night before, but the herd of two hundred persisted in returning to the beach. By Monday afternoon at least seventy-two were dead. Isn't that over one-third?

On September 21, 1975, a headline in the *Birmingham Post Herald* read: "State River Disaster Trilogy Cost Millions." Then also, in large print, an Editor's Note read: "During the past seven months major mishaps have occurred on the Warrior, Coosa, and Tennessee Rivers in

Alabama." What about the two large dams that broke, the last one in 1976, causing loss of life? And *those dams were government-built!*

You should just see all the newspaper articles filed here telling about floods throughout the world. Dover, England, reported their worst Channel storm in twenty-nine years. But then, in 1976, what a terrible drought hit Britain.

REV 8:9 reads: " . . . and the third part of the ships were destroyed." What about the Bermuda Triangle? Disasters are escalating as evidenced by reports:

December 22, 1976: "Five million gallons of oil spill into fish-rich Atlantic waters. The tanker, Argo Merchant, was ripped in half by 20-foot waves Tuesday, spewing more than 5 MILLION GALLONS OF HEAVY CRUDE OIL INTO SOME OF THE ATLANTIC OCEAN'S MOST PRECIOUS FISHING WATERS."

December 1976: "Los Angeles ship-blast cause sought. The Sansinena, a 510 foot ship, was blasted by a gigantic explosion." December 1976 again, Cairo, Egypt: "The 10,500 ton Patra was headed for Egypt with 4–500 passengers crew when the 23-year-old ship caught fire hours after leaving Saudi Arabian port Jaddah, Thursday, and sank early Friday. Ahram newspapers said in early morning (Monday) editions, 350 persons were dead and 85 were missing. Most of the Egyptians were returning from Moslem pilgrimage to Saudi Arabia."

December 1976 again: "Oil slicks peril three states, Pennsylvania, New Jersey and Delaware. The Coast Guard said 1,335,000 gallons of light Arabian oil leaked from the 771 foot tanker Olympic Games about 15 miles from Philadelphia. Oil has already washed up on the shores of Chester, Pennsylvania, in New Jersey and in Delaware."

December 1976 again: "Off the coast of Connecticut

2,000 gallons of oil spill from the Liberian tanker Oswego Peace, which began leaking from the ship's fuel tanks, affected several miles of the Eastern Shore of the Thames River."

Now, on January 12, 1977, a carrier and a Liberian freighter collided. Messina dateline: "The U.S. carrier Franklin D. Roosevelt and the Liberian freighter Oceanus collided in rough seas Wednesday, in the Straits of Messina, between the Italian mainland and Sicily, port officials said."

January 13, 1977: "Twenty-three were killed as freighter rams boatload of servicemen. Barcelona, Spain, a Spanish freighter sliced into a launch ferrying more than 100 American sailors and Marines back to their ships from shore leave at 2:00 A.M., Monday. Twenty-three men died and others were feared missing. Huddled in bitter cold in the open launch, they saw the freighter only seconds before the collision: 'Two seconds later we were in the water.' 'We went down like somebody had pulled the plug,' said a Marine from Reebling, N.J."

On January 4, 1977, a loaded fuel tanker was reported missing: "Boston: The Canadian and U.S. Coast Guards launched a search Monday for a missing tanker carrying 8 million gallons of heavy fuel oil from England to Providence, R.I. This ship was never found or any survivors, all were lost."

January 21, 1977: "Honolulu, the tanker Irenes Challenger, a 633 ft. vessel, a Greek owned ship, buckled and broke in two in moderate seas, after passing through some stormy weather. She was carrying 4.5 million gallons of light crude oil from Venezuela to Japan."

Again, on January 29, 1977, an oil-laden barge spilt its load in a canal: "Boston: A barge carrying 3.5 million gallons of #2 fuel oil ran aground at the entrance to Cape Cod

Canal Friday night rupturing four of its 19 tanks and dumping an undetermined amount of oil into the frozen sea."

Here is another one about fish: "January 19, 1977: Cold holds tight grip over the East." Then, later, a paragraph states: "In Michigan, state officials expressed fears of a massive fish kill unless heavy snow and ice melted on the state's 11,000 lakes. THE ICE COVER WAS BLOCKING SUNLIGHT NEEDED BY UNDERWATER PLANTS TO PRODUCE THE OXYGEN THAT FISH MUST HAVE TO LIVE."

Here is one from New Orleans (February 26, 1978): "Tiny parasite is responsible for fish deaths. 'A microscopic parasite . . . NOT MAN'S ECOLOGICAL INROADS . . . caused thousands of game fish to die in Southeastern Louisiana waters,' wildlife biologists said." From another paragraph: "'This particular parasite thrives in cold water, and we've been having record low temperatures lately,' said a spokesman for the Louisiana Wild Life and Fisheries Commission."

Here is one from October 3, 1978:

Landslide Crushes Ocean Resort Homes

> A huge landslide jolted the fashionable seaside resort Monday sending at least 24 expensive homes slithering down hillsides and leaving others tottering precariously on crumbling cliffs. Geologists had no immediate word on what caused the slide, nor could they say when the ground would stop moving. Firemen and policemen were in the neighborhood immediately, comforting people and evacuating them. The hillside oceanview homes were valued at between $175,000 to $300,000 by Lu Wrede of a Laguna Beach realty firm.

Who controls the weather? Isn't that another way in which God is carrying out what was prophesied in REV 8:9 when it said: "And the third part of the creatures which were in the sea, and had life, died . . . ?" Sure that was just a small happening in Louisiana, but we only hear about those things that are close to our country, yes, once and a while also in other parts of the world. I heard recently that sardines had left a certain area where they had been very plentiful for many years *and the cause was unknown.*

Do we need further proof that this vision portrayed what had been prophesied many years ago? Are we awake, watching, and learning our lesson?

All those ships in trouble or sunk during December 1976 and on January 29, 1977! And what about all those offshore oil wells in trouble and the oil going up in flames and all the oil that was lost from those ships in trouble or sunk? This is oil that was and is needed because of the energy crisis. More about this later as we give the interpretation of the third vision, the sounding of the third trumpet.

What really was the important message of this vision? The messenger from God, the man that appeared so suddenly and said, "*I would advise you to keep right on going. We have had a terrible landslide,*" et cetera. All this makes it appear that the second vision is an announcement by God's messenger that the second trumpet has sounded in heaven. REV 8:8: " . . . a great mountain, burning with fire, was cast into the sea. . . . " This is a mountain of trouble brought upon man with the fire of God's wrath, because of sin.

THE LION HAS ROARED

Last week, when I finished typing the preceding section, the thought came again: *Who am I that I should write this book?* So the book was put aside; there were so many things that had to be done. *But* now, three days later, I am back at it again. Why? Praying for guidance and that God's will be done, I was just going to wait until I could see, know, what He would have me to do.

We went to the hospital yesterday to say farewell to Henry's oldest sister. She had suffered a severe stroke and was going to be taken back to her home in Detroit. Naturally, there were many thoughts on our minds as we retired and as we talked about some of the difficulties that they would face, both during the trip and on arrival home. Since she is eighty-five years old and we at this time were in our eighties, we may never see her again, here on earth. Commending them all to God's care, I went to sleep. *But* a dream, that was so much like the one that I will be typing up next has convinced me that I must continue with this writing. If I left it there, put it aside, discontinued writing, then it would be following *my* will. If I continue writing until something happens to stop me, to keep me from doing so, then it would be God's will. It is His will that I pray will be done.

Now, after taking the things from my file and arranging them, I find where already, in May 1969, I was shown what I ought to do *but did not.* Because of this, the following dream must also be included, although I have been very reluctant to do so. Wouldn't it be wrong if not all was told? Oh, how wonderful it would be if I could write about the faith, love, sincerity, joy, and happiness of all believers in Jesus Christ, our Savior. But nothing of that nature was shown. Only God's anger and judgments were shown to me, because of sin in the world. We have no control over our dreams. Only God can give us the true interpretation of them, when we pray and leave the whole matter up to Him. It seems that the interpretations that I am given begin to unfold after awakening suddenly from each dream or vision and then not being able to go back to sleep. The interpretations are not always complete, as you will see, at times.

AMOS

This dream began with my entering an assembly. I heard the voice of a man reading the Scriptures. A pastor was standing beside him.

I went directly to them and asked, "Why is *he* reading?"

The pastor answered, "Because whoever reads should do so slowly, distinctly, and with expression."

I asked, emphasizing certain words, "And haven't I been reading thus, *slowly, distinctly,* and with *expression?*"

The pastor hesitated. I waited for an answer. Then he said, "Yes, Mrs. Miller, you have." He made no further comment, nor did he ask me to read, so I left and went into a room where the Sunday School and Bible classes were assembling.

A teacher was seating pupils and other people about her. She had all the teaching material.

I asked, "Why do you have *all* the material?"

She answered, "Because you have not been coming regularly."

I asked my children to come and go with me, as the teacher gave me some of the material. Some children hesitated. After class we were called to gather for the General Assembly, the closing period. We sat there and waited and waited for the pastor. Finally he came, but only to walk through the assembly without a word. So we were still waiting for his return. Finally I arose and said, "Let us arise and pray the Lord's Prayer together and be dismissed." Some arose; others just sat there and looked as if to say, "We don't have to do what you say." I and those others that stood up prayed. We were finishing when the pastor entered from the rear. He looked as if he had just washed up, combed his hair, and put on a clean shirt, but no coat. *How he looked at me and I at him!* Suddenly I was outside, alone, and there, directly in front of me, was written in large letters, and I heard: "AMOS 3:1–10."

I had never read the book of Amos with any special interest, but you may be sure that as soon as time permitted that morning I read and reread AMOS 3:1-–10. It reads:

> Hear this word that the LORD hat spoken against you, O children of Israel, against the whole family which I brought up from the land of Egypt, saying, You only have I known of all the families of the earth: therefore I will punish you for all your iniquities. Can two walk together, except they be agreed? Will a lion roar in the forest, when he hath no prey? will a young lion cry out of his den, if he have taken nothing? Can a bird fall in a snare upon the earth, where no gin is for him? shall one take up a snare from the earth, and have taken nothing at all? Shall a trumpet be blown in the city, and the people not be afraid? shall there be evil in a city, and the LORD hath not done it? Surely the Lord GOD will do nothing, but he revealeth his secret unto his servants the prophets. The lion hath roared, who will not fear? the Lord GOD hath spoken, who can but prophesy? Publish in the palaces at Ashdod, and in the

palaces in the land of Egypt, and say, Assemble yourselves upon the mountains of Samaria, and behold the great tumults in the midst thereof, and the oppressed in the midst thereof. For they know not to do right, saith the LORD, who store up violence and robbery in their palaces.

At this time I could not understand what God was showing me in Amos, but later the text had a very important meaning.

Symbols and Their Meanings
1. Assembly, a man reading, pastor stands by: By tradition and the ministry, only men have a voice in church matters in so many churches.
2. Why is *he* reading?: My question, because I know what God's word says about this matter.
3. Whoever reads must do so *slowly, distinctly,* and with *expression.* Their reasoning: men are better qualified.
4. Haven't I read thus?: Haven't I attended church services regularly, been faithful at Sunday School teachers' meetings and training courses, organized and conducted Christian Growth Institutes, been a witness for Christ? Many other women have also done so.
5. Hesitated, then said, "Yes, Mrs. Miller, you have.": Thus reluctantly he had to admit it. (In a letter to the Commission on Theology and Church Relations I had just recently also proven this.)
6. Kept right on reading: Ignoring what God's word says, that God is not a respecter of persons.
7. Assembly: They have talked about my position on this matter at conferences, et cetera. Now it goes before the convention again.
8. Teacher wants to keep the material and the children:

They want to continue in the practice of: "Let your women keep silence in the churches."

9. Teacher says, "You have not been coming regularly: Meaning that I haven't studied and thus do not understand God's word as well as they do.
10. Does give me some of the material: Yes, I was allowed more privileges than most women. I was even on the Board of Education and during a vacancy was in full charge of Vacation Bible School.
11. Classes dismissed: The matter goes from committee and conferences to the convention again.
12. Waiting for the pastor: Waiting for their decision.
13. Being in the general assembly: All members are waiting for the decisions of the convention.
14. The pastor passes through but does not stop to dismiss the pupils: The ministry tries to hold out on the matter. It has gone from one convention to another.
15. I ask for prayer and dismissal: No doubt many women prayed.
16. Some do so: others would not: General stand of the members.
17. Pastor appears and looks as though he had just washed up, combed his hair, and put on a clean shirt but no coat: Convention had cleared itself of this matter and decided that there is nothing in God's word that could hinder the women from voting and taking a more active position in the work of the church.
18. The way the pastor looks at me and I at him: He wants to say, "Now are you satisfied?" and I want to say, "Well, finally you have dropped the tradition of men and are accepting the teachings of the Word of God."
19. I hear and see in large letters: "Amos 3:1–10": There are still pastors and churches that will not give the women a voice in church matters, thus verse 3: "Can

two walk together, except they be agreed?"; verse 9: " . . . and the oppressed in the midst thereof"; and verse 10: "For they know not to do right, saith the LORD, who store up violence and **robbery in their palaces.**" Is it robbery to take away the rights of some of the church members, the women?
20. AMO 3:8: "The lion hath roared, who will not fear: the Lord GOD hath spoken, who can but prophesy?": I am to tell what happened and to continue teaching what God's word says, which also includes answers to this matter.
21. AMO 3:9: "Publish in the palaces": I am to continue writing about personal experiences.

For several years my husband had been very disturbed about the lack of women's rights in the church. He never got anywhere, though, when discussing it with pastors and other people. The women had no vote in church matters, yet young working women and widows were expected to contribute to everything that the men voted on. They had no representation at the meetings. Sometimes there would be only ten to fifteen men attending a "voters' meeting," as it was called. Time and time again my husband would remind me that God is not a respecter of persons, with God it is neither Jew nor Greek, bond nor free, *male nor female* (GAL 3:28). Christ died for all.

A church paper once carried a dialogue between two men. One of the men asked a question: "Do women have the right to vote in congregational meetings, or don't they?" It continues: "Realizing that this question called for a cautious answer, I replied simply 'Yes and No.' (You can't become much more cautious than that.)" End of quote. Now this really upset me. God does not give cautious or lukewarm answers. With Him the Bible says,

Yea, yea or Nay, nay: "But let your communication be, Yea, yea; Nay, nay: for whatsoever is more than these cometh of evil" (MAT 5:37).

Another portion of the dialogue creates another issue: "And although they don't have a right to vote, they can serve as resource persons and voice their opinion. You see, the church recognizes, as it always has, that women, too, are members of the body of Christ, that they are indeed God's gifts to the church," et cetera. But are women invited to those meetings? *No!* God's gifts? A gift can be used, stored away, given away, or destroyed. By now, you can imagine how I felt. Women are members of the church.

Still another issue is discussed in the dialogue in the paper: "Women should learn in silence and all humility. I do not allow women to teach or have authority over men. They must keep quiet, for Adam was created before Eve. And it was not Adam who was deceived and broke God's law." Then the author quoted 1CO 14:34–35: "Let your women keep silence in the churches: for it is not permitted unto them to speak; but they are commanded to be under obedience as also saith the law. And if they will learn any thing, let them ask their husbands at home: for it is a shame for women to speak in the church." Now I had all I could take. He didn't quote verse 36: "What? came the word of God out from you? or came it unto you only?" I ask, therefore, *Did the Word of God come from men, and is it given to men only?* Here, we have another example of what happens when a verse or verses are taken out of context. That whole chapter deals with verse 40: "Let all things be done decently and in order." Oh, so much more could be written about this. If the women are being left out, are things being done decently and in order?

Here also is the matter of Adam being created first. It was mentioned several times in this article. Then, also mentioned was "God's creative scheme." Let me ask: Who are we that we can determine God's creative scheme or plan?

God gave Adam a command (GEN 2:17): "But of the tree of the knowledge of good and evil, thou shalt not eat of it: for in the day that thou eatest thereof thou shalt surely die." Then, in GEN 2:18, 21–23, *God* formed Eve, the woman. When Eve was tempted by the devil, ate of the fruit, and gave some to Adam, he did eat. Shouldn't he, instead, have **repeated God's command:** "*Thou shalt not eat . . .* " and then *not done so?* Thus was he so superior? No, he also took and ate.

In EPH 5:22 we read: "Wives, submit yourselves unto your own husbands, as unto the Lord." This says "*wives* and husbands." That is a rule for family life, not church life. Christ is *the head of the church; men* are not *heads of the church.* We are *all members* of the *body,* and *there should be no schism among us.* Read EPH 1:22: "And hath put all things under his feet, and gave him to be the head over all things to the church"; EPH 5:23–24: "For the husband is the head of the wife, even as Christ is the head of the church: and he is the saviour of the body, Therefore as the church is subject unto Christ, so let the wives be to their own husbands in every thing"; 1CO 11:3: "But I would have you know, that the head of every man is Christ; and the head of the woman is the man; and the head of Christ is God"; 1CO 12:1: "Now concerning spiritual gifts, brethren, I would not have you ignorant"; 1CO 12:12: "For as the body is one, and hath many members, and all the members of that one body, being many, are one body; so also is Christ"; 1CO 12:25: "That there should be no schism in the body; but that the members should have the same care one for another"; and COL 1:18: "And he is the head of the body, the church: who is the beginning, the firstborn from the dead; that in all things he might have the preeminence."

Here is another one (EPH 4:14–16): "that we henceforth be no more children, tossed to and fro, and carried about with every wind of doctrine, by the sleight of men, and cunning craftiness, whereby they lie in wait to deceive; But speaking the truth in love, may grow up into him in all things, which is the head, even Christ: From whom the whole body fitly joined together and compacted by that which every joint supplieth, according to the effectual working in the measure of every part, maketh increase of the body unto the edifying of itself in love." Note that it says "whole body." Is God a respecter of persons? No!

Here is a wonderful example to prove that God is not a respecter of persons. To *preach the gospel* is a direct command from God. MAR 16:15: "And he said unto them, Go ye into all the World, and *preach the gospel to every creature.*" It says "EVERY CREATURE," doesn't it, and "Go?" Do we pay attention to God's *commands?* Good, well, let us study a few of them, throughout this writing.

We are New Testament believers. The coming of the Savior had been prophesied many times. *But* to whom was this good news that he was **about to arrive** given first? It tells us in Saint Matthew and Luke. It was not to a man. When Joseph learned about his wife Mary's pregnancy before they had come together, he wanted to put her away. But while trying to decide what to do he was advised by an angel not to do so, because "that which **is conceived in her** is of the Holy Ghost. And SHE SHALL BRING FORTH A SON, AND THOU SHALT CALL HIS NAME JESUS: FOR HE SHALL SAVE HIS PEOPLE FROM THEIR SINS" (MAT 1:18–20). In LUK 1:31 Mary was informed that she would be the mother of Jesus **prior to conception:** "And, behold, thou **shalt conceive** in thy womb, and bring forth a son, and shalt call his name JESUS." Joseph learned about Jesus after conception, Mary before conception, by the Holy Spirit. This shows that the gospel message, the good news of the Savior's arrival, was first given to a woman. Yes, it says "Jesus," thus the Savior. Thus the first good news or gospel message in the New Testament was *first given to a woman.*

Another woman to realize the truth about Jesus was Elizabeth. In LUK 1:41–43 we read: "And it came to pass, that, when Elizabeth **heard the salutation of Mary,** the babe leaped in her womb; and Elizabeth was filled with the Holy Ghost: And she spake out with a loud voice, and said, Blessed art thou among women, and blessed is the fruit of thy womb. And whence is this to me, that the **mother of my Lord** should come to me?"

Who was the first to praise God for this good news? Mary. . . . Read LUK 1, beginning with the forty-sixth verse. Thus it was not Joseph that thanked God first that the Savior was to come, but Mary.

Now let us turn to the last chapter of the book of Matthew. What are the three most wonderful words that you have ever heard, important words that we can ever say, will ever hear? Yes: *"He is risen."* Why? He *is* risen. 1C15:17: "If Christ be not raised, our faith is in vain, we are yet in our sins"; and 1CO 15:20: "BUT NOW IS CHRIST RISEN FROM THE DEAD AND BECOME THE FIRST FRUITS OF THEM THAT SLEPT." There would be absolutely no hope for us if He had remained in the grave. Saint Paul said (1CO 15:19): "If in this life only we have hope in Christ, we are of all men most miserable." Now *to whom was this gospel message, the good news of the living Savior, first given?*

Please picture this with me. See *the women* as the day is beginning to dawn hurrying to the tomb of Jesus. Suddenly one remembers and asks, "Who will roll away the stone?" Ah, but it is already rolled away when they get there.

GO

" . . . Fear not ye: for I know that ye seek Jesus, which was crucified. He is not here: **for he is risen** . . . " (MAT 28:5–6). Thus mark this: an angel gives the gospel message to women first, not to John and Peter, as they went to the tomb. Then follows an invitation from a messenger sent by God, an angel (verse 6): "Come see where the Lord lay."

Next, in verse 7, is a direct **command** by the angel, yes, a command unto **WOMEN**. "Go, quickly and tell His disciples that he is risen from the dead." What wonderful news the women were able to carry to the disciples . . . yes, the gospel. Is that right? It sure is; God's word says so.

First, let us look at the command "Go." You heard that before in MAR 16:15, when Jesus spoke to the eleven. He gave the command, also to the eleven, in MAT 28:19: "Go ye therefore," et cetera. In MAT 28 we find it twice, the command given to women, "Go," and again in LUK 20:11 to Mary Magdalene. This calls for action: *do something*. Then "QUICKLY," that is right. They are not to wait until they accidentally meet one or more of the disciples; they are sent directly, to "GO QUICKLY" AND TELL His disciples, MEN, the good news that He is risen.

HE IS RISEN

The women receive *more good news* (MAT 28:7): "And go quickly, and tell his disciples that he is risen from the dead; and, behold, he goeth before you into Galilee; there shall ye see him: lo, I have told you." THERE SHALL YE SEE HIM. Yes, the angel, a messenger from God, even confirms it by saying, "LO, I HAVE TOLD YOU." GOD, THROUGH HIM, HAS GIVEN THE ORDERS." "GO . . . QUICKLY . . . AND TELL, HE IS RISEN." You can see that as He gave special mission commands to both men and women, God is not a respecter of persons.

This should be enough to convince us all, but read on. MAT 28: 9: "And as they went to tell his disciples, behold, Jesus met them, saying, All hail . . . . " Thus Jesus appeared first to women. And they came and held Him by the feet and worshiped him. Then said Jesus unto them (MAT 28:10): "Be not AFRAID." Just think about this. They are not to be afraid to "GO, TELL MY BRETHREN." Thus we have a second "GO" in the same morning, this one by Jesus, for women to carry the good news or gospel message "HE IS RISEN" to MEN.

BUT THAT IS NOT ALL

In JOH 20 we read that Peter and John went to the tomb. We read nothing about an angel or Jesus greeting *them* or giving *them* a message or command. In JOH 20:11–16 we read that two angels and then Jesus spoke to Mary Magdalene about delivering the good news of the resurrection to the disciples. Yes, it was years before the full meaning of all that happened that day was fully understood by me. I was taking in all that I heard from *men*.

Jesus also gave Mary Magdalene the first message about His ascension (JOH 20:17): "Jesus saith unto her, Touch me not; for I am not yet ascended to my Father: but go to my brethren, and say unto them, I ascend unto my

Father, and your Father; and to my God, and your God." Here is the THIRD COMMAND IN ONE DAY, "GO TELL," UNTO THEM, *TO MEN.*

How did the disciples receive the message? Even though the women had been sent by God and Jesus? We have the answer in MAR 16:14, where we read: "Afterward he appeared unto the eleven as they sat at meat, and upbraided them with their unbelief and hardness of heart, because they believed not them which had seen him after he was risen." Thus how could the pastor that was answering the questions say what he did about women's rights? Wasn't he going along with the tradition of men, instead of the Word of God? For all these many years the ministry and the church taught and went along with the tradition of men. I remember a time when the men went to the Lord's supper first. Before I ever married, my dad and I would talk about this division in the church. This custom of men going to the Lord's supper first finally ended.

Thus in the vision *the man reading the Scriptures and the pastor standing beside him* showed the tradition of men. My asking, "Why is *he* reading?" shows how I felt about the matter. The pastor answering, "Whoever does so must read, *slowly, distinctly,* and *with expression,*" was to say that men are better educated and qualified. My answer to this would be: "Many, many more women attend Bible classes, Christian Growth Institutes, and even now, since they have electric washers, driers, refrigerators, vacuum cleaners, frozen and prepared food, they can have so much more time to devote to the Lord's work." Isn't that probably why God has given us so many conveniences? Or should women be kept silent to some extent and spend their time at the TV, bridge parties, golf courses, bowling alleys, et cetera? Shouldn't they be working with the pastors on the different boards? One church paper recently showed a whole row of pictures of men, eight or nine of them, serving on different church boards and *only one woman.* Why must Bible classes be divided by sex when many women are as well versed, familiar with, and firmly grounded in the Bible as some men?

Well, as I said before, by the time I had finished reading that article, I had had enough. It really stirred me into action. I wrote a five-page single-space, article to the Commission on Theology and Church Relations, quoting one Bible passage after another. Yes, I had *WRITTEN SLOWLY, DISTINCTLY and WITH EXPRESSION.* In the dream, the pastor had to admit it. I had written to *men* only, without significant returns, and as in the dream, they kept right on reading.

The teacher, keeping most of the children and the material, showed what they would like to do. Finally, I was given some material. Yes, I must truly say that in real life I was granted many more privileges than most women. I was a member of a School Board and Superintendent of the Primary Department (but I was told not to advertise that) and was given permission to have complete charge of Vacation Bible School during a vacancy. One pastor even reminded me that I had been given special privileges, but as I wrote to the commission, I told them that as Esther pleaded for her people, thousands of years ago, I was now pleading for my people, the women of the church who, to some extent, were still in bondage of a type.

Then *going into a general assembly and waiting for the pastor* was the waiting for a decision from the convention on this matter. *When he came through and didn't stop,* it showed that the convention was still trying to hold out, as they had been doing from one convention to another.

In the dream, when *I suggested that we arise and pray,*

some would not, but others did, showing that some women still accept what they hear and they had been taught: let your women keep silence in the churches. But many women had prayed about this matter.

Now the *pastor came in again, looking as though he had just washed up, combed his hair, and put on a clean shirt, but no coat.* Well, I had written to the Commission on Theology in August. The synodical convention was the following May. Now the appearance of the pastor in the vision showed that the commission had finally cleared themselves of this matter, and it was decided *that there is nothing in the Scriptures that could hinder a woman from voting and holding offices on boards and committees of the church* (*Lutheran Witness,* June 1969).

After all, these many years the church had gone along with the tradition of men. Thus in the vision I was shown what was about to happen at the next convention. The pastor looking after his own well-being is also a picture of the pastors and churches that still do not allow their women a voice in church matters. This is also happening in some other denominations. Another denomination's church paper has come out with the headline: "___ [name withheld] Grapple with Place for Women in Christianity." It seems that these articles confirm that God has taken care of these things that have troubled me and my husband for many years. AMO 3:1–10!

Several pages back I asked the question: "Do we pay attention to God's commands?" Before we end this section let us consider some of them again. It seems important to do so. MAT 28:16: "Then the ELEVEN disciples went away into Galilee, into a mountain where Jesus had appointed them." Verse 19, His command unto them: "GO YE THEREFORE AND TEACH ALL NATIONS," et cetera. So the command to the eleven apostles was to "teach all nations."

As Mark puts it (MAR 16:14–15): "Afterward he appeared unto the ELEVEN. And he said unto them, GO YE INTO ALL THE WORLD AND PREACH THE GOSPEL TO EVERY CREATURE." In both instances no women were present. The *preach command* to the apostles was unlike the ones given to the women. The women were told to "GO AND TELL," pass a message to the disciples or brethren. (They happened to be the apostles, one named Peter.)

Read carefully and study 1CO:12 again. Saint Paul states it plainly. 1CO 12:28: "And God hath set some in the church, first apostles, secondarily prophets, thirdly teachers, after that miracles, then gifts of healings, helps, governments, diversities of tongues"; 1CO 12:4: "Now there are diversities of gifts, but the same Spirit"; 1CO 12:5: "And there are differences of administrations, but the same Lord"; and 1CO 12:6: "And there are diversities of operations, but it is the same God which worketh all in all." Thus men and women doing Kingdom Work can be a blessing to a congregation, because there is a diversity of gifts from the Holy Spirit.

But women as preachers? *No!* Did you notice that whereas Jesus' disciples were told to *go and preach,* we have not found or read in the Scriptures that women were told to "go, preach"? Why are some women so anxious to do so? Because this is happening so frequently in the world today, it seems necessary to study the Scriptures more closely on this issue. What an interesting study it is!

In my concordance it states that "woman" is mentioned 102 times, "women" 44 times, in the New Testament. That is not counting the women called by other terms such as "lady," "sister," "daughter," "kinswoman," et cetera, or those mentioned by name: Elizabeth, Mary, Anna, Mary Magdalene, Dorcas, Martha, Eunice and Lois,

Phebe et cetera. Nowhere did I find where one was told to "go preach." No women were present at the Transfiguration, the Last Supper, or Jesus' ascension, when the great commission was given to the disciples to go and teach (MAT 28:18–20).

Also in the New Testament prophetesses are mentioned. In LUK 2:26 there is Anne, in ACT 21:9 one man's four virgin daughters prophesied and in REV 2:20 there is the seducer Jezebel, who called herself a prophetess. But prophesying is not preaching. To prophecy is to predict, foretell, or forecast the future.

PHI 4:3 says: "And I entreat thee also, true yokefellow, help those **women which laboured with me in the gospel,** with Clement also, and with other my fellow labourers, whose names are in the book of life." We read also in ROM 16:1–2: "I commend unto you Phebe our sister, which is a servant of the church which is at Cenchrea: That ye receive her in the Lord, as becometh saints, and that ye assist her in whatsoever business she hath need of you: for she hath been a succorer of many, and of myself also." Other women helpers in Christ mentioned in ROM 16 include Priscilla, Mary, Junia, Narcissus, Tryphena, and Julia. Thus I find nothing in the Scriptures that could keep women from likewise being servants of the church by being members on some of *those many "boards."* Also, too many pastors are serving on them, et cetera instead of leaving "the ninety and nine, and goeth into the mountains, and seeketh that which is gone astray" (MAT 18:12).

The same synodical convention that extended suffrage to its women and the right to participate on various church boards, according to the June 1969 *Lutheran Witness,* also defined that women were not permitted to preach or to hold such offices in which they could exercise authority over men. Again it seems that God, working through the convention, reaffirms the guidance given by His word using both text and examples.

HO-HO-HO

Another Christmas season has come and gone. For many Christmas is a time of rejoicing, a time to give thanks and praise and honor and glory to God for His wonderful gift to man, His beloved Son, Jesus Christ. Picture in your mind that first Christmas night: shepherds are in the field, and suddenly above them the sky becomes bright and beautiful, it opens, and out of heaven appears an angel saying those wonderful words: "Fear not." If you've heard them once, you will know what a wonderful, peaceful feeling comes upon you. Words are just too inadequate to describe it. God willing, I hope to write about it someday.

"And the angel said unto them, Fear not: for, behold, I bring you good tidings of great joy, which shall be to all people. For unto you is born this day in the city of David a Saviour, which is Christ the Lord" (LUK 2:10–11). Knowing that we have a living Savior should bring peace, joy, and happiness to every heart. "And suddenly there was with the angel a multitude of the heavenly host praising God, and saying, Glory to God in the highest, and on earth peace, good will toward men" (LUK 2:13,14).

Yes, they were praising God and giving glory to God, *but how many people at Christmas celebrations, as we know them today,* give glory and praise to God? Yes, there are some Christians that do. *But do the majority?* Many activities are called Christmas, but Christ is almost or completely left out of it. Would Jesus attend the many Christmas parties that should honor His birth? His name is used. *Would He be present with a Santa Claus and a clown?* Is it only non-Christians that attend these activities? Is it true that many people are religious but not Christian? Isn't this being *lukewarm? God warns us about being lukewarm* (REV 3:16).

Satan has been active . . . very, very busy ever since the first people were tempted in the garden of Eden. In GEN 3 we read how he misquoted God and planted doubts in the woman's mind. God had commanded Adam (GEN 2:16–17): "And the LORD God commanded the man, saying, Of every tree of the garden thou mayest freely eat: But of the tree of the knowledge of good and evil, thou shalt not eat of it: for in the day that thou eatest thereof thou shalt surely die." They would already be dead to that *perfect life with God of peace, joy, happiness, plenty, in that beautiful garden,* but they would also, some day, die.

As Satan spoke to Eve, what did he say? Did he repeat God's words? No! He made it sound so different as he said (GEN 3:1), " . . . Yea, hath God said, Ye shall not eat of every tree of the garden?" There was only the tree of knowledge of good and evil that God had forbidden to them, but Satan made it sound so different, sound like more, when he used the word "every."

To this day, planting doubts and using questioning lies are *some of his tricks.* He doesn't need to go after his own, the lost; he already has them. It is the Christian and those who seek a better life, searching for peace of mind and happiness, that he often bombards with doubts, and in subtle ways he tries to win them over to himself.

Here is a question on Christian practice that can raise doubts. How do we know when Jesus was born? Where does it say that He was born on December 25? The Bible, God's word, does not say or command us to celebrate Jesus' birth, nor does it say that we should celebrate His resurrection. If God wanted us to do so, it would be commanded, just as the children of Israel were told to keep, and remember, the Passover.

Yes, planted doubts. *Must God tell us, "It is Jesus' birthday; now celebrate it"?* If I had to tell my family, "It is my birthday; now celebrate it," where would their love for me be? Shouldn't we, out of grateful hearts, set aside a day *or more* to remember Jesus' birth and also His resurrection? Where is our love or gratitude if we must be told to do so? They also teach that no gifts should be given. The matter of gift giving today appears to have gotten out of hand. People are going to the extremes, and it is not being done in the spirit that it should be done. Gifts are no longer given to remind people of God's wonderful gift, His Son. Gift giving is a wonderful practice if done with love, in remembrance of God's love.

Some teach "no gift giving, no greeting cards, et cetera," but their leaders visit foreign countries, giving expensive gifts to the rulers and receiving gifts from them. One especially that I read about was a gold medal for the Lion of the Tribe of Judah. The recipient was Haille Selassie, because he claimed to be that Lion. *That title belongs to Jesus only.* Read it in REV 5:5. Where was this man's knowledge of the Bible? Yet some claim they alone understand it and know it better than most people.

When the angels sang, "Glory to God in the highest," wasn't that setting an example for us? I admit we should not only give Him glory when celebrating His birth, but the Scriptures teach us that we should also be witnesses of Him, of His love and mercy and grace. Shouldn't it be celebration of His birth, his life, His sacrificial death on the cross, and finally His victory over sin, death, and the devil? That includes His birth and resurrection. Our witness should be especially loud and clear to the true meaning of His birth when the earth, the worldly, are celebrating it in such as pagan way. Even so, many of the so-called Christians and believers do not witness to the true meaning of Christmas. All too many follow the ways of the world. All too many are so busy preparing for the day that there is little or no time for the true preparation for and meaning of Christmas to fill their hearts with the true joy and happiness that it should produce. If and when we celebrate Jesus' birth in a Christian way, aren't we witnessing to others about our faith in Him? Didn't He say, "Ye shall be witnesses of me"? See ISA 43:10, JOH 15:27, and ACT 1:8. Shouldn't the church doors be open on Christmas day and all believers come together to praise and honor and worship, God? LUK 2:11: "For unto you is born this day in the city of David a Saviour, which is Christ the Lord." Yes "glory to God in the highest, and on earth peace, good will toward men" (LUK 2:14). What business does a boar's head, yule log, or puppets have at a Christmas celebration of Jesus' birth?

A cartoon picture, but I think it really showed a true picture, in the *Birmingham Post Herald* before Christmas one year had the following caption "Following yonder star." It showed the star that much of the world was following, especially our U.S.A. At the top of the picture there was a huge star on which in lights appeared: "OPEN 7 DAYS A WEEK." Glittering rays were all around it. "MERRY CHRISTMAS," in a half-circle, was printed in glittering letters below it, then the same words in other languages. On the roof of the entrance were the words: "OPEN 'TIL MIDNIGHT." Standing on the roof of the entrance was a huge figure of Santa Claus. There he stood, with his arms outstretched, as if to say, "Come unto me, all ye people, and I'll relieve you of your money; come and buy. Sarah will give something to you, so will the Joneses, et cetera. You've got to buy something for them. The time is getting short. You'll be tired tonight, so you'll be able to get a good night's rest." Masses of people were going under the roof. On the inside there would probably be a Santa Claus, and parents would be taking their children to see him and to talk to him. The cartoon gives an idea of what commercializing Christmas is all about.

Isn't it Satan that is "Ho-Ho-Hoing," with his belly shaking like jelly, when he can draw so many away from the spiritual meaning of Jesus' birth and turn their hearts to the thoughts of material things? Isn't it a *lie* to tell children that there is a Santa Claus, he lives at the North Pole, and each year he comes to bring them gifts? What does that Santa, a man sitting there listening to kids talk, care about them or what they want? It is a lie. Businesses are making profits that pay him to live a lie. Isn't Santa also drawing the love away from the parents unto himself, because the children believe that he brings their gifts? Have you read all the many Scriptures that mention lying and the judgments that are pronounced upon liars? Here is just one, REV 21:8: "But the fearful, and unbelieving, and the abominable, and murderers, and whoremongers, and sorcerers, and idolaters, and all **liars,** shall have their part in the lake which burneth with fire and brimstone: which is the second death." Shouldn't this cause a person to be afraid to lie in any way? Jesus when speaking to the multitude said (MAT 5:37), "But let your communication be, Yea, yea; Nay, nay: for whatsoever is more than these cometh of evil." There is no straddling the fence with God. We are either for Him or against Him; we either tell the truth or we lie.

Making children think that Santa Claus is bringing their gifts also steals from the parents the love and honor and joy and thankfulness due them. Why? Because the parents love their children and so often make sacrifices so as to give the children things that they desire, even going into debt, sometimes for months, so as to see the happy faces of the children on Christmas morning. Yes, it is a lie that Santa brings the gifts. Satan is using the business world to make us more covetous from year to year. Already in October they begin to display their wares, and Santa Claus can rejoice with more and more "Ho-Ho-Hoing," with his belly shaking like jelly, because he can draw the minds of people away from the Christ child.

No, I have not forgotten all the good and charitable things that are done by Christians during the Christmas season. I read an article just recently in which one recipient of this charity said that he was grateful for what folks did for him, but that he received everything at once, at Christmas time, and then he was forgotten during the rest of the year. He felt so alone and forgotten.

Isn't it grieving the Holy Spirit when minds are so taken up with material planning and *material things* when they should be filled with the joy and happiness of the spiritual side of Christmas? God's word says "grieve not the Spirit" in EPH 4:30: "And grieve not the holy Spirit of God, whereby ye are sealed unto the day of redemption."

Where is the pastor that would dare to speak out against Santa Claus? Did you read where there was one and the congregation tried to expel him? Are these things the reason I was shown, in a vision written about in the next section, a dozing ministry, a resting church ... *lukewarmness of the people?*

And what about Easter, the great Resurrection Day of our Lord and Savior, Jesus Christ? Because He lives, we also have the hope of eternal life with Him. We will not have eternal life with Easter bunnies, eggs, and new clothes. Satan is again rejoicing, because the hearts and minds are again drawn away from Jesus. The true meaning of His Resurrection Day is weakened or lost altogether. Straddling the fence again, wanting to go along with God and His plans, but not willing to give up the worldly doings of the sinful, is being **lukewarm.**

CHRISTIAN OR ONLY RELIGIOUS?

Jesus said, as we read in MAT 5, beginning with verse 17, "Think not that I am come to destroy the law, or the prophets: I am not come to destroy, but to fulfill. For verily I say unto you, Till heaven and earth pass, one jot or one tittle shall in no wise pass from the law, till all be fulfilled. Whosoever therefore shall break one of these least commandments, and shall teach men so, he shall be called the least in the kingdom of heaven: but whosoever shall do and teach them, the same shall be called great in the kingdom of heaven. For I say unto you, That except your righteousness shall exceed the righteousness of the scribes and Pharisees, ye shall in no case enter into the kingdom of heaven." Yes, he came to set an example for us and said, "Follow me." *But* oh, how we fail, yes, how miserably we fail! That is why He also became our Savior. That is why He lived, suffered, and died for us, so that we might have forgiveness of all our sins.

Now if you had been condemned to death and someone would take your place, spare your life (which no human being would do), and that person died but you were set free, wouldn't you be forever grateful? You couldn't show your gratitude to him, but you could to his family. Wouldn't you feel that you *owed* it to them, that you could never repay them for what he had done for you? That is what Christians owe to God, to Jesus Christ our Savior, to His followers, believers, and children. If we, then, with the guidance of the Holy Spirit, try to live a life according to God's word and do His will as much as possible, admitting our sins of commission and omission and asking His forgiveness, then only can we be called his children and also bear the name Christian.

1JO 2:4–6 says: "He that saith, I know him, and keepeth not his commandments, is a liar, and the truth is not in him. But whoso keepeth his word, in him verily is the love of God perfected: hereby know we that we are in him. HE THAT SAITH HE ABIDETH IN HIM OUGHT HIMSELF ALSO SO TO WALK, EVEN AS HE WALKED." Aren't many of the people that are listed as church members only religious and not Christian? How many of them are church members? How many of them are Christians? Of course only God knows the true answer.

What about all those people that were involved in the Watergate scandal and other scandals, all those receiving bribes, all those making excess profits, all those lying about their financial status, all those going on expensive junkets at the taxpayers' expense, the doctors and lawyers that charge exorbitant fees, the directors and boards of hospitals that pile up huge profits at the expense of the sick and the dying and Medicare so that they can build more hospitals when we read in the papers that they are not needed? There are already too many empty beds in the hospitals. And what about those that sold contaminated wheat out of New Orleans to foreign countries? And I could go on and on. *Are they all outside the church?* According to what we read in the first chapter of John, can we call them Christians? Aren't they only religious ... lukewarm? Read the following. Isn't the answer therein? 2TI 3:1–5: "This know also, that in the last days perilous times shall come. For men shall be lovers of their own selves, covetous, boasters, proud, blasphemers, disobedient to parents, unthankful, unholy, Without natural affection, trucebreakers, false accusers, incontinent, fierce, despisers of those that are good, Traitors, heady, highminded, lovers of pleasures more than lovers of God; Having a form of godliness, but denying the power thereof: from such turn away."

Are not the following things examples of covetousness? One man, before leaving office (and this was reported in the *Birmingham Post Herald* on December 1, 1976), visited London, Moscow, and Mexico City, at a cost to the taxpayers of more than $130,000 for his party. Quoting: "Nor was it clear why he felt it necessary to take a party of 45 to Moscow, including three members of his own family, and wives of several other department officials, who went along for the ride." December 3:

> As we learned this year, while another one and his colleagues were surveying bases in such exotic locations as Las Vegas, Paris, and the Virgin Islands, the military augmented the $75.00 a day they receive while abroad, by picking up the tab with taxpayers' dollars for their expensive meals, lodging, entertainment, and liquor, and even their laundry bills. Bear in mind, of course, that congressmen have voted themselves a taxpayer funded salary of more than $44,000 a year, plus numerous fringe benefits, and a staff whose salaries cost taxpayers another $200,000 a year for each congressman.

February 20, 1977:

> Voting to adjourn, the $12,000 pay raise goes into effect.

Just think of the people in the United States that don't even get the first $12,000 a year. Isn't this extreme covetousness?

Don't some of the people that our legislators are supposed to represent have to pay ninety cents or more, some out of their minimum-wage salary, in order to go to work while the legislators are riding chauffeur-driven limousines to work? With so many people out of work I sometimes wonder how some of these people in Washington, yes, and elsewhere, that are supposed to represent the people can sleep at night. What if Jesus should suddenly come? Read AMO 8.

Thousands and thousands are out of work, getting by on handouts, others just barely making a living, others having to pay such high taxes that only enough is left for their necessities, and thousands never get a vacation. Nursing homes are so expensive that many cannot afford to go there. Big businesses are piling up profits for themselves and their stockholders at the expense of those that need homes and a few conveniences to make life a little more enjoyable or easier. Here is another example. What about the people that are being paid, say, five, six, seven, eight, nine, or ten dollars an hour or more and spend so much time at the water cooler or in the rest rooms, smoking their cigarettes? Sure, a glass of water or a drink of water from the fountain is all right, but to meet a friend there and chat, should that be? Should three, four, or more times a day be spent in the rest rooms smoking cigarettes? Shouldn't a person give "an honest day's work for an honest day's pay"?

About twenty years ago, some land was advertised in the papers, and when my husband and I went to look at it, we decided it would be ideal for a garden. It was only ten minutes away. We purchased the property and we planted many different kinds of vegetables. We bought a large freezer to stock the vegetables. Even though it was hard work, we enjoyed those good homegrown vegetables. We also *froze* many to use during the winter months. About the third year we began to notice something. Both of us were beginning to have swollen knuckles. What could be causing that? Yes, we were *both* starting to suffer from arthritis. Then one day as I was freezing beans, blanching them, and pouring off the water, I noticed how green it was. Then, when I was blanching the corn, the water that was being poured out was yellow. So *what had* we been doing? We were *pouring off and losing something. Vitamins? Were we only getting leftover vitamins?* It was decided that we would not rely on frozen foods as much as we had been doing. Some fresh fruits and vegetables would have to be added every day. Just think of how much frozen food is consumed now. *Do we hear warnings about the same?* Besides the freezing, what about all the additives in foods? Is it any wonder that there is so very much arthritis nowadays? Ours was very much retarded and thereafter caused very little trouble. The markets publish no warnings. Big business benefits if they are silent about the alleged hazards of frozen foods. Pain relievers are used for arthritis instead.

What about all the millionaires and the idle rich? Here is what Saint Mark says in the tenth chapter, verses 23–25 *and they are Jesus' words:* "And Jesus looked round about, and saith unto his disciples, How hardly shall they that have riches enter into the kingdom of God! And the disciples were astonished at his words. But Jesus answereth again, and saith unto them, Children, how hard is it for them that trust in riches to enter into the kingdom of God! It is easier for a camel to go through the eye of a needle, than for a rich man to enter into the kingdom of God." *Why?* we wonder. Well, how did they obtain their riches? What are they doing with them, et cetera?

Did you notice the word "doing"? Do we have to do

something? We are saved by grace, through faith. Read LUK 6:45–47: "And why call ye me, Lord, Lord, and do not the things which I say? Whosoever cometh to me, and heareth my sayings, and DOETH THEM, I will shew you to whom he is like." Also read MAT 7:22-24: "Many will say to me in that day, Lord, Lord, have we not prophesied in thy name? and in thy name have cast out devils? and in thy name done many wonderful works? And then will I profess unto them, I never knew you: depart from me, ye that work iniquity. Therefore whosoever heareth **these sayings** of mine, and DOETH THEM I will liken him unto a wise man, which built his house upon a rock." What are *these sayings?* Just read MAT 5,6, and 7.

Thank God that we are saved by grace, but that is no license for us to do just as we will, live just any way, and then rush to Him and ask Him to forgive us. That is cheapening grace, belittling what Jesus did for us. If we could do just about anything that we want to do, then why do we read (this is in the New Testament) 1CO 6:9–10: "Know ye not that the unrighteous shall not inherit the kingdom of God? Be not deceived: neither fornicators, nor idolaters, nor adulterers, nor effeminate, nor abusers of themselves with mankind, Nor thieves, nor COVETOUS, NOR DRUNKARDS, NOR REVILERS, NOR EXTORTIONERS, SHALL INHERIT THE KINGDOM OF GOD"? 2TI 3:1–5 puts it this way: "This know also, that in the last days perilous times shall come. For men shall be lovers of their own selves, covetous, boasters, proud, blasphemers, disobedient to parents, unthankful, unholy, Without natural affection, trucebreakers, false accusers, incontinent, fierce, despisers of those that are good, Traitors, heady, highminded, lovers of pleasures more than lovers of God; Having a form of godliness, but denying the power thereof: from such turn away." ***This is "having a form of***

Godliness" . . . LUKEWARM! Yes, we are saved by grace, as we read in EPH 2:8–10: "For by grace are ye saved through faith; and that not of yourselves: it is the gift of God: Not of works, lest any man should boast." *But what we so seldom hear is the following verse* (10): "For we are his workmanship, created in Christ Jesus unto good works, which God hath before ordained that we should walk in them."

Have you ever noticed how important some little words are, *if, but, for, is, what,* and others? Just recently I heard on a TV program EZE 18:4, but only the last half of the verse: " . . . the soul that sinneth, it shall die." Then the man said, "All have sinned and so *the soul that sinneth it shall die." But what he neglected to do was read the next verse.* Yes, it starts with a "but": "But if a man be just, and do that which is lawful and right, and hath not . . . ": then it lists three verses of sins. Verse 9 then says: "Hath walked in my statutes, and hath kept my judgments, to deal truly; he is just, he shall surely live, saith the Lord GOD." Thus verse 4 was quoted out of context, for verse 20 says: "The soul that sinneth, it shall die. The son shall not bear the iniquity of the father, neither shall the father bear the iniquity of the son: the righteousness of the righteous shall be upon him, and the wickedness of the wicked shall be upon him." Then there is another "but," et cetera. So, going back to EPH 2:10: "For we are his workmanship, created," yes, created, "in Christ Jesus unto good works," unto good works, "which God hath before ordained that we **should** walk in them." WHICH THE LORD HATH BEFORE ORDAINED THAT WE *SHOULD* WALK IN THEM. The word is not "may" or "can," but **"should."**

The Third Trumpet

THE THIRD VISION

One night in February 1973, I saw a vision of a large man sitting in a large chair, a recliner, dozing. At his right, kneeling beside the chair, with her arms on the arm of the chair and her head resting on her arms, was a woman dressed in black. At the left front of the chair and facing it was a shadowy figure. I stood to the right front of the chair. The man stirred. He was about to get his foot caught between the chair and footrest, so the shadowy figure and I pulled it away. The man stirred again and this time exposed his whole rear end, naked. The shadowy figure tried to cover the man with a dazzling white sheet. He uncovered himself; again the shadowy figure tried to cover him, then the third time, but each time it was useless. I left in a hurry and went out a side door and joined a group of really happy people, as it seemed, in a large open field.

Suddenly two stars were there in the sky in front of us, connected, weaving all over the sky. While we were watching this, four stars appeared forming a square, not connected except for the top and bottom rods, or sticks, which were connected by a bar going through the center, on which was a large, fiery red ball. As this was very slowly moving downward, a bomb crossed in front of it. A shadowy cloud was to the right, and the outlines of several things behind the cloud were visible.

I said, "I'm going to tell Mother."

A voice said, *Don't wake him up.*

I answered, "I think he is already awake."

As I went into the house, Mother was sitting in a rocking chair. I must have told her what I had seen, because she answered, "Watch it, child; it could be for a sign."

I answered, "I know it is." Then I went out the door. Here came the two stars, headed right toward me. Now they turned, curved up to the northeast, turned again, and came down as one star with a fiery tail, down behind the trees, where the water was. Suddenly I was awake. There was no more sleep that night.

Symbols and Their Meanings
1. Man in a recliner, dozing: Attitude of the ministry during the last days.
2. Woman in black, kneeling beside the chair: The church.
3. Shadowy figure standing to the left front: Holy Spirit or angel.
4. Man restless: REV 3:17.
5. Uncovers rear end: REV 3:17.
6. Happy people: Other Christians, also from other denominations.
7. Two stars: Old and New Testaments, which have been warning, all these many years, what would take place during the latter days, and also, as one star announced the birth of Jesus to the Wise Men, now two stars are announcing that soon will be his second coming.
8. Four stars: Four angels holding back the winds until the elect of God have been sealed on their foreheads.
9. Four rods or sticks: The winds, judgment to follow.
10. Fiery ball: The end.
11. Bomb: War of Syria, Jordan, and Egypt with Israel.
12. Shadowy cloud and objects: Judgments yet to follow.
13. Voice from above saying, *Don't wake him up*: God's message—don't write to the ministry.
14. "I think he is already awake": My mistake.
15. Mother in the rocking chair: The church of which I was a member.

16. "Could be for a sign": Attitude of the church— "could be."
17. "I know it is": Only God could give such a vision.
18. Two stars coming toward me: To alert me to what was about to happen.
19. Large star with a fiery tail: REV 8:10
20. Waters: REV 8:11

LUKEWARMNESS IN THE CHURCH

God does not change. We are being forewarned, being reminded, that what was prophesied about the latter days is happening. Jesus, speaking in LUK 21:34–36, said, "And take heed to yourselves, lest at any time your hearts be overcharged with surfeiting, and drunkenness, and cares of this life, and so that day come upon you unawares. For as a snare shall it come on all them that dwell on the face of the whole earth. **Watch ye therefore, and pray always,** that ye may be accounted worthy to escape all these things that shall come to pass, and to stand before the Son of man." There is no straddling the fence with God. We are either for Him or against Him; we are either hot or cold. He will not accept *lukewarmness,* as you will see as you read.

In order to "watch" we must know what to look for. We need God's word to inform us and alert us so that we will not be misled—for instance, when we hear "peace, peace" when there is no peace. When Saint John was writing the Book of Revelation, he was instructed to write to the *seven churches* (REV 1:20). God was not pleased with some of the things that were happening within the churches. When we read about the last one, the church of the Laodiceans, we tremble. *Why?* Because God says, "I know thy works, that thou art neither cold nor hot, I would that thou wert cold or hot, So then because thou art lukewarm and neither cold nor hot, I will spue thee out of my mouth." In other words, he would *get rid of her. What a terrible judgment!* Three times the words "cold nor hot" are used and then those terrible words: "I will spue thee out of my mouth." *Shouldn't this make us stop and think and examine ourselves?*

Some years ago, a Mrs. Reinhardt conducted mid-week Bible classes at the YMCA in Birmingham, which my husband and I attended. We were studying the Book of Revelation. She said that the seven churches represented seven dispensations and explained that she believed that we were living in the time of the seventh or the Laodicean period.

In REV 3:17 we see why God, with the first part of the vision of February 1973, was showing me the condition of the ministry and the churches of today. Was God preparing me for what I was to see, *that same night,* in the vision of the stars? Was the vision telling me that the third trumpet had sounded in heaven? The flaming star falling on the water is the clue that caused me to look in the Bible for interpretation. I found REV 8:10: "And the third angel sounded, and there fell a great star from heaven, burning as it were a lamp, and it fell upon the third part of the rivers, and upon the fountains of waters; and the name of the star is called Wormwood . . . "

There was nakedness in my vision. In REV 3:17 I found: "Because thou sayest, I am rich, and increased with goods, and have need of nothing; and knowest not that thou art wretched, and miserable, and poor, and blind, and naked." I had seen nakedness; that was the second clue. It reminded me of verse 18: "I counsel thee to buy of me gold tried in the fire, that thou mayest be rich; **and white raiment, that thou mayest be clothed, and that the shame of**

thy nakedness do not appear . . . ," et cetera.

If it should ever happen that you also see a vision, one with such heavenly appearances, you will never forget it. But just as wonderful is this: that even before I arose, the Holy Spirit was already unfolding the interpretation. Not completely, as you will see.

The woman kneeling beside the chair is another clue. The church is generally portrayed as a woman. Who, then, was the man? The ministry. The shadowy figure to the left front of him was the Holy Spirit or an angel, trying to cover him. Thus it was brought to my attention what I had read in verse 18: "And white raiment that thou mayest be clothed and the shame of thy nakedness do not appear."

The dozing man is the ministry; the woman in black is the church, but she should, as the bride of Christ, be dressed in white. With her arms resting on the side of the chair and her head resting on her arms, she is the picture of the church, sitting (she was kneeling) at the feet of the ministry, taking it all in, maybe seldom speaking up. When I did speak up once, another church member said, "We pay the pastor to teach and explain the Bible to us; he is the one that we should listen to." Is this the general attitude of the church members? I don't know. The vision points to the same.

In some church services the sermon text is read from the Bible and then it is never heard or referred to again. Story after story, experience after experience, of pastors or others, "I" this and "I" that, take the thoughts away from the *Word of God.* Lukewarm? *Halley's Bible Handbook* mentioned that God's word is intended to be the centerpiece of church services and concludes that if church leaders had heeded early warnings, the church might not have encountered the appalling corruption it has experienced through the ages.

And what about the pastors who, Sunday after Sunday, present object lessons before the sermon? An umbrella or brick, balloon, or flower, et cetera, is used as an object to get children's attention for a spiritual lesson. Isn't this risk *OUT OF PLACE? There is ONLY ONE HOUR,* probably, all week to worship God in the sanctuary, to hear *His Word, to give praise and honor and thanks to Him, but time is spent using earthly, perishable subjects instead.* Isn't a child much more apt to receive a Bible lesson and God's word as they were written? Isn't the faith of children often much stronger than that of adults? They don't question and doubt the Word. When Jesus spoke, as we read in Matthew, Mark, and Luke, he used the faith of a little child as an example for adults (LUK 18:17): "Verily I say unto you, Whosoever shall not receive the kingdom of God as a little child shall in no wise enter therein." It was the children's faith that he was talking about. If object lessons are used to teach children, they should be selected carefully for simple understanding. Here are examples of object lessons that show the risks taken when object lessons are used.

During one service, the pastor had a balloon. He held it out with a pin to a little boy and asked him to stick the pin in the balloon. The child would not accept it and looked up at his mother. She shook her head no. That child had been taught not to be destructive, and he remembered. The pastor wanted to teach the lesson of breaking the law, but it didn't work that way. Some child that had not been paying strict attention could go home and say, "Pastor thinks that it is all right to break a balloon; he told Billy to do it."

Here is another example. One Sunday it was eyeglasses and eyeballs. The sermon ended: "When with our eyeballs we observe the beauty of God's creation we can and should praise Him," et cetera. One member's six-year-old daughter later at the dinner table said, "Mother, now you can have all the highballs you want." Her mother was shocked and asked, "Chris, what do you mean? What made you say that?" She answered, "The pastor said so this morning. He said we can praise God with them." When object lessons are used, it should be during a class period so that the children have a better opportunity to discuss and to understand.

What about a pastor dramatizing Bible characters such as John the Baptist, Joseph, Pontius Pilot, Zacharias, Simon, and Judas Iscariot? Quoting from a county weekly: "Dressed in tunic and sandals, donning make-up, a false beard and wig for his monologue." Quoting further: "I felt that this would be a new *VEHICLE* [the italics are mine] in which I could reach people." WHAT? A *CRUTCH* FOR THE HOLY SPIRIT? HAS THE HOLY SPIRIT BECOME SO WEAK THAT IT CANNOT REACH THE MINDS AND HEARTS OF PEOPLE WITH THE WORD OF GOD? Others read such as this and will follow this pastor's example. Will not people be entertained by drama instead of being strengthened, enlightened, admonished by the Word of God? "Let no corrupt communication proceed out of your mouth, but that which is good to the use of edifying, that it may minister grace unto the hearers. And grieve not the holy Spirit of God, whereby ye are sealed unto the day of redemption" is what the Bible teaches (EPH 4:29–30).

And what has happened to the children's Bible study time? *They use the time for crayons, scissors, and listening to an explanation of how to do something or make things.* As a Sunday School teacher in an organization where I *had* to use such things, I saw the children come in on a Sunday morning and ask, "What are we going to make today?" Their minds were drawn away from the Bible lesson and turned to the material things.

Just think this over: *ONLY an hour or less ONE DAY A WEEK is given to study God's word in a Sunday School class, and so much of the time is given over to visual aids, drawing, coloring, making bookmarks, valentines, and the like. Has the Holy Spirit become so weak that it cannot reach the hearts and minds of people, through THE WORD OF GOD? Does it need all kinds of crutches and aids to help it along? Isn't this doubting the power of the Holy Spirit? Isn't it being LUKEWARM?*

What about the churches that include adoration of the host during the Lord's supper, statues of saints and the Rosary in their worship? Where is such commanded in the Bible? So much more could be said about all this, but here are several quick references. Paul and Peter could truly be called saints, but did they allow men to fall down before them? ACT 10:25–26: "And as Peter was coming in, Cornelius met him, and fell down at his feet, and worshipped him. But Peter took him up, saying, Stand up; I myself also am a man." ACT 14:15: "And saying, Sirs, why do ye these things? We also are men of like passions with you, and preach unto you that ye should turn from these vanities unto the living God, which made heaven, and earth, and the sea, and all things that are therein."

No wonder that we read in REV 3:17: "BECAUSE thou sayest, I am rich, and increased in goods and have need of nothing." But verse 18 tells us: "I counsel thee to buy of me gold tried in the fire, that thou MAYEST by rich, and white raiment that thou MAYEST be clothed, and the shame of thy nakedness do not appear." No wonder, then, that the shadowy figure in the vision was trying to cover the dozing man, the ministry, with a dazzling white sheet. Lukewarm, yes, showing *so little faith in the power of the Holy Spirit.* And the woman beside the chair, *THE*

CHURCH, promotes all these kind of activities. The ministry does not correct or admonish the members *that they should trust in the Lord and not lean on their own understanding.*

Another lukewarm attitude, in some churches, is how the Lord's supper is observed. A weakness comes to our attention when we read 1CO 11:29. This should really make one tremble: "For he that eateth and drinketh unworthily, eateth and drinketh damnation to himself, not discerning the Lord's body." The previous verse, verse 28, says: "BUT LET A MAN EXAMINE HIMSELF AND SO LET HIM EAT OF THAT BREAD AND DRINK OF THAT CUP." Do some of those children or even some adults that attend the Lord's supper know how to do this, and is it done before partaking of the Lord's supper? In some churches there is little said, so little preparation, along this line.

Since the words of greatest importance are "FOR THIS IS MY BLOOD OF THE NEW TESTAMENT WHICH IS SHED FOR MANY FOR THE REMISSION OF SINS"(MAT 26:28), each person who has a different position in life: father, mother, son, or daughter, lawyer, politician, doctor, scholar, worker, official, executive, teacher, businessman, and so on should ask himself, *"Do I truly repent of my sins?"* Have I been truthful, honest, kind, loving, forgiving, et cetera, regardless of my position in life? We should judge ourselves using the ten commandments, one by one. Have I loved God above all things and my neighbor as myself? Only then must we humbly confess that because of our sinful nature there have been sins of commission and omission and that we need the *forgiveness of sins. Jesus did suffer and die for us, shed His blood for us, that we might have that forgiveness.*

Next we should also ask ourselves whether we have

that good and honest intention, with the help of the Holy Spirit, *to amend our sinful ways.* Wouldn't there be a big change in the church and also in the world if all church members that partake of the Lord's supper would truly repent of their sins and then *not go back to the activities of the world with its lusts, covetousness, and other sins?* Perhaps we should read and ponder those words again, as recorded in 1CO 11:26–30: "For as often as ye eat this bread, and drink this cup, ye do shew the Lord's death till he come. Wherefore whosoever shall eat this bread, and drink this cup of the Lord, unworthily, shall be guilty of the body and blood of the Lord. But let a man examine himself, and so let him eat of that bread, and drink of that cup. For he that eateth and drinketh unworthily, eateth and drinketh damnation to himself, not discerning the Lord's body. For this cause many are weak and sickly among you, and many sleep."

We have reviewed some of the "lukewarmness" of pastors, the ministry, and the church. There is more to the vision. The first half of the vision showed a dozing man in a large chair, a woman kneeling beside him. The second half, the heavenly part, showed two moving stars, rods, bomb, and combining stars. The interpretations follow.

THE FIRST HALF OF THE VISION

The man was about to get his foot caught between the footrest and the seat. The shadowy figure, the Holy Spirit, and I pulled it away. That pointed to the times that I, by the guidance of the Holy Spirit, took a firm stand and spoke up when things were being planned or happening within the church that were not according to God's word or would not set a Christian example. Then *the shadowy figure tried to cover the man's nakedness.* NOTE THIS: he was not completely naked, only his rear end, so THERE IS A FORM OF GODLINESS.

This then brings us to REV 3:17: "Because thou sayest, I am rich, and increased with goods, and have need of nothing; and knowest not that thou art wretched, and miserable, and poor, and blind, and naked." Christians today have seminaries, Bible colleges, churches, missionaries in foreign countries, Evangelism and mission boards, church services (sometimes several times a week), Bible classes, deacons, elders, study groups, mission societies, choirs, and brotherhoods. Yes, we have all kinds of conferences, oh so many, and retreats for pastors and laymen, crusades, prayer meetings, revivals, et cetera, and they are usually very well organized. Isn't that demonstrating *increased with goods and have need of nothing?*

In the same verse we read: "and knowest not that thou art wretched and miserable." Why? Because they just don't know what else to do to get people to come and go along with them, to join them. They already have suppers, bazaars, entertainments, home tours, bingo, puppet shows, bridge parties, camping trips, and so on.

The next word is "poor." Poor in preaching and teaching the whole will of God, as we read in 2TI 4:1–3: "I charge thee therefore before God, and the Lord Jesus Christ, who shall judge the quick and the dead at his appearing and his kingdom; Preach the word; be instant in season, out of season; reprove, rebuke, exhort with all longsuffering and doctrine." What is happening in so many denominations is what we read in verses 3 and 4: "For the time will come when they will not endure sound doctrine; but after their own lusts shall they heap to themselves teachers, having itching ears; And they shall turn away their ears from the truth, and shall be turned unto fables."

God wants all men to come to the knowledge of the truth, and that includes *that He is also a righteous God and hates sin.* It cannot be just a public confession that one accepts Jesus Christ as Lord and Savior. There must be a true repentance of sin, a new birth, as the Bible tells us, and turning *away from all past sins, a true resolve to live a more Christ-like life.*

Now "blind." That is easy to understand. It is just not being able to see the weaknesses, the lukewarmness that has crept into churches. It already started in Bible times, but just read how strongly they were told of their weaknesses. Just read the seven letters to the seven churches in Revelation and the epistles in the New Testament.

The next word in verse 18 is "naked." All the lukewarmness, everything that should be done but is neglected because of the "*busyness*" of the church, all is open, seen, naked, before God. HEB 4:13: "Neither is there any creature that is not manifest in his sight: but all things are naked and opened unto the eyes of him with whom we have to do." Doesn't that include churches? What do we read in REV 3:18? "I counsel thee to buy of me gold tried in the fire, that thou mayest be rich; and white raiment, that thou mayest be clothed, and that the shame of thy nakedness do not appear; and anoint thine eyes with eyesalve, that thou mayest see."

What! Does it read "to buy"? It surely does. Haven't we been told that salvation and God's love and mercy and grace are the free gifts of God? They are, and they pertain to the spiritual life. Just think what it cost Jesus, the Son of God, to redeem us. Didn't He leave His heavenly home to be born of a woman, to be born under the law, to redeem them that were under the law? He became subject to Mary and Joseph, obedient to God and man. He was tempted like as we, called a wine bibber and a glutton, chief of devils, and finally was scourged, spit upon, and crowned with thorns and suffered the terrible agony of crucifixion. Didn't it cost Him His life to redeem us? And yet salvation is free. Why, then, *buy?* That is the physical side of the picture. Man does not like to part with money or his worldly doings. The churches, no doubt, would not like to part with their worldly doings. Dramatizing, object lessons, puppet shows, story after story, "I" this and"I" that, instead of staying with a text, the true Word of God. Why visual aids instead of using the precious little time that we have for teaching the Word of God? Why suppers, bazaars, et cetera, et cetera? How many would be willing to give up their worldly activities and visit the sick, the needy, the aged, the orphans, the discouraged, the burdened, the sorrowful and bereaved? How many would be willing to help wherever help is needed? Yes, there are some Christians that do, *but they are so few.* When we buy something, we give up something, generally money, but why not give up some of our God-given time and use it in the ways that His word directs? Jesus' life was a life of gold, tried in the fire, but He came out victorious. Oh, how we fail! God's word, the Bible, is pure gold, tried in the fire. Many have tried to destroy it, but it is now stronger than ever.

The next words, REV 3:18, read: "That thou mayest be rich." We should not be rich in the *"busy-ness" of the church,* not in the worldly activities that have been added to it, but in the riches of God, a greater acceptance of His word and teachings, a closer walk with Him, and the true riches of a more Christ-like life.

Then "and white raiment." ISA 1:18: "Come now, and let us reason together, saith the LORD: though your sins be as scarlet, they shall be as white as snow; though they be red like crimson, they shall be as wool." God is ready and willing to forgive us our past sins if we repent and walk in a newness of life. Why white raiment?

Now the words: "That thou mayest be clothed, and that the shame of thy nakedness does not appear." Consider 1PE 1:13–16: "Wherefore gird up the loins of your mind, be sober, and hope to the end for the grace that is to be brought unto you at the revelation of Jesus Christ; As obedient children, not fashioning yourselves according to the former lusts in your ignorance: But as he which hath called you is holy, so be ye holy in all manner of conversation; Because it is written, Be ye holy; for I am holy." And the last part of REV 3:18: "And anoint thine eyes with eyesalve, that thou mayest see." Hasn't there been a certain blindness within the ministry and the church? There must have been, or we would not have such a warning to the churches as we read in the last book of the Bible, the Book of Revelation. Remember the warning? REV 3:15–16: "I know thy works [notice it says **"works,"**] that thou art neither cold nor hot: I would thou wert cold or hot. So then because thou art lukewarm, and neither cold not hot, I will spue thee out of my mouth." What a terrible judgment . . . a separation from God!

REV 3:19: "As many as I love, I rebuke and chasten: be zealous therefore, and repent." Yes, and *repent.* Verse 20 continues: "Behold I stand at the door and knock. . . . " That is what it says: "I STAND AT THE DOOR AND KNOCK." But shouldn't Jesus be on the inside, be in and with the church? Must *He stand outside and knock?* It is very late. He has been patient, He has delayed his coming, but NOW He is standing at the door and knocking.

Please do not think that I am entirely against meetings and church gatherings. Some meetings are necessary so that everything is done decently and in order. Some meetings are very important. Read ACT 1:15–26. ACT 6:1–8 also tells of an important meeting that took place and the wonderful fruits that it produced. Seven men were chosen not to sit around in meetings but to be appointed to have charge over certain business. We read about one of them, Stephen, full of faith and power, who did great wonders and miracles *among the people.* Verse 10 of ACT 6 says: "And they were not able to resist the wisdom and the spirit by which he spake."

An occasional dinner or meal to which the *whole congregation* has been invited is also not out of place. The church should be like a large family or relationship; thus an occasional family reunion is all right. It can renew and strengthen the family togetherness. Today's trouble is that so much of it is overdone and poorly managed, and because of that, it also loses some of its effectiveness. One experience that I definitely remember was when a reception was being held for all new members that had joined the church during the past three months. The occasion was also to help celebrate the sixtieth anniversary of a couple, the wife of which was also celebrating her ninetieth birthday. Of course, all these people were in the receiving line. So what happened? The children all rushed to the tables and selected the choicest food. I almost cried when my ninety-year-old friend finally did get to the tables and there was so little food to choose from. Going to the tables where the children had eaten, I was shocked to see how much was left uneaten and would end up in the garbage bucket. This is not the way I was brought up. Where were the parents? I suppose greeting the new members and honorees, but this is just one example of how children are turned loose today and there is so little supervision or training to preserve the purpose of gatherings.

At a different church, I attended three monthly night

family dinners. At each one of these dinners the pastor and his wife, the pianist and her husband, and the Bible Class teacher and his wife went aside into a Sunday School room to eat. Where were their children? The rest of the congregation also divided into little groups or even families alone. Well, they could have eaten alone at home. There I stood; it made it difficult for me to know what to do. Which group should I try to join? I had met so few of them during the six months that I had lived in that community. Finally one family invited me to join them.

These incidents show that if the events had been planned, something had gone wrong. They were almost a waste of time, because the reason for having such affairs had *been lost along the way.*

Why enumerate all these weaknesses in the church of today? To show that there does exist a lukewarmness. Man does not want to acknowledge the full power of God and His word but thinks that he must add some of his knowledge and thoughts to it. All the wisdom of the world, added and put together, could not measure up to the wisdom of God.

Isn't it time to wake up, be prepared? What time is it? We need to remember REV 3:15–18.

THE HEAVENLY PART

In the third vision, you recall, as I left the scene of the dozing man and the resting woman I went out a side door and joined a group of very happy people and we were going through a meadow or field together. Then began the heavenly part of the vision.

Two stars appeared, and they were connected. It must have been nighttime. The stars were weaving back and forth and all around in the sky. What were the stars and this activity? The stars were angels or witnesses of the Old and New Testament, which have warned and are warning that what has been prophesied will soon happen. The final judgment day is rapidly approaching. The warnings have just about reached around the world with the help of radio messages in so many different languages, TV, crusades, the *Bible for New Readers,* the easier to understand *Living Bible,* and even travelers and missionaries. As one star alerted the Wise Men to the coming to earth, the birth, of Jesus Christ, our Savior, so also these two stars may be to alert mankind that the second coming of Jesus will soon take place.

Then while I was watching these two stars, four stars appeared, high in the sky. There were four rods or sticks between them as they formed a square, but they were not connected to the stars. The top rod and the bottom rod were connected by a rod going down through the center of the square. A huge red ball was on that center rod. The vision recalls REV 7:1: "And after these things I saw four angels standing on the four corners of the earth, holding the four winds of the earth, that the wind should not blow on the earth, nor on the sea, nor on any tree. And I saw another angel ascending from the east, having the seal of the living God: and he cried with a loud voice to the four angels, to whom it was given to hurt the earth and the sea, Saying, Hurt not the earth, neither the sea, not the trees, till we have sealed the servants of our God in their foreheads."

But this four-star thing was coming slowly toward us. It was still high in the sky. As it was slowly moving down from the sky, a bomb passed across it. So you see, it was already in close view. The four stars were the four angels that had been holding back the winds. The four rods were the four winds or the four judgments or punishments that are yet to come when the four remaining trumpets sound. The fiery ball was the fiery destruction that will come at the end. Because this was moving slowly, does it mean that the time is approaching, no longer being held back, that the tribulation period has already begun? And the bomb? Well, that was one thing that I just did not understand at the time, only that we know that there shall be wars and rumors of wars before the time approaches. Just a few months later, though, I was also shown what the bomb was to tell me.

When I said, "I'm going to tell Mother," it was then I heard. *Don't wake him up.* I answered, "I think he is already awake." As the interpretation of the first half of the vision became known to me, I had to learn that the big man in the chair is dozing, not fully awake, and that he represented some of the ministry.

As I went into the house to tell Mother, she was sitting in a large rocking chair. I don't remember telling her about our experience, but she said, "Watch it, child; it could be for a sign." I answered, "I know it is." Here we have the woman, the church, taking it easy in the rocking chair, and saying, "It *could* be for a sign." Yes, that is the questionable looks or comments when the experience of the vision is told to members of a church. Since this is a woman, resting on a chair, it again means the church, and because it was my mother, it was also the congregation to which I belonged at the time. Thus this congregation is included with all the rest, with all the others. According to the vision, God is not pleased, and He tells us so in the Book of Revelation as I have already said.

Leaving Mother, I went out the door that went to the east. There, again, were the two stars, alone, and they were coming toward me about treetop height. Then they turned toward the northeast, going somewhat higher. They turned again, came down as one large star, toward the earth, toward the South, and now it has a large fiery tail. It came down to earth behind the trees where the water is. No doubt I was to be alerted to the movement of the stars, because they came toward me before going higher and turning to come down as one large star that had a fiery tail. It was the latter that opened the door to the interpretation of what I had seen. I woke up with such a suddenness and again looked about me. I was not in the open field; I was in my room. No more sleep that night. It was that falling star that made me realize that I had read something in the Bible about a star falling on the waters, in the Book of Revelation.

As soon as breakfast was over, I looked in my Bible. Yes, there it was, REV 8:10–11: "And the third angel sounded, and there fell a great star from heaven, burning as it were a lamp, and it fell upon the third part of the rivers, and upon the fountains of waters; And the name of the star is called Wormwood: and the third part of the waters became wormwood; and many men died of the waters, because they were made bitter." I believe that this vision of the falling star shows that the third trumpet of the seven angels has sounded (REV 8:2). This was prophesied, though, that it would happen, and John, on the Isle of Patmos, was told to write it, and thus we have the prophecy in the Book of Revelation.

As the Holy Spirit prompted and brought to Peter's mind on the day of Pentecost what had been prophesied already in the Old Testament by the prophet Joel, wouldn't he also bring it to someone's mind somewhere and with visible signs of some kind? This is that which was prophesied and shown to John on the Isle of Patmos? We can go directly to the Scriptures and read what was prophesied. We can compare what is being told us or what we are reading with that which was prophesied many years ago. Of course, we must remember that many things written in the Book of Revelation are symbolic and so we must search the Scriptures further in order to understand their meaning.

If a star should fall to earth from heaven, not everyone on earth would or could see it. Is God going to leave it unannounced? Wouldn't it somehow, in one way or another, be made known: *this is that which was prophesied?* So "the burning star fell upon parts of the waters and they became Wormwood." What are the waters? Waters are voices or words, in this case earthly or worldly *voices.* We read about the living waters in JOH 4:10–13. These are words to live by in order to inherit eternal life. In EZE 43:2 we read God's voice was like a noise of many waters. In REV 14:2 we read: "And I heard a voice from heaven, as the voice of many waters, and as the voice of a great thunder: and I heard the voice of harpers harping with their harps." In JER 9:15 we read of a different kind of water: "Therefore thus saith the LORD of hosts, the God of Israel; Behold, I will feed them, even this people, with wormwood, and give them water of gall to drink." In JER 8:14, " . . . for the LORD our God hath put us to silence, and given us water of gall to drink, because we have sinned against the LORD." Thus "waters" are words, in this case also worldly water, and as we have read, they will become wormwood, bitter. As the waters become bitter, so the words, the reports that man will hear, read, see on TV, become to him "bitter." And some men will even die because of them. Bitter words? Bitter reports? Some have already said that God is dead. If they have no faith in Him, their soul is already dead to His mercy and grace and truth. They do not have the living water. Look at Watergate, other scandals, the oil embargo, higher and higher food prices, utility and transportation costs, the dollar going down so low in value. People are afraid to leave their homes at night because of what might happen to themselves or to their homes while they are away. Bitter, because of higher and higher taxes, rising unemployment, higher and higher food prices, shortage of gas for home and factories at times. Many people would not vote, bitter because of all that happened in recent years. Can't you hear them say, "Will this never end?" Not only in this country, but all over the world, the people are rising up and making themselves heard, because they are bitter over what is happening in their countries. REV 8:11: " . . . and many men died of the waters, because they were made bitter." Yes, think of the deaths that have taken place in some countries, because the people are making themselves heard and so their rulers have them imprisoned or send the armies out after them and many of them die.

Just think of what it costs to buy a home. What about doctor bills and hospital expenses? Many people, all over the world, are not receiving medical care because they cannot afford it or, in some cases, it is not available. What about the bitter words of miners and farmers lately? So many people become bitter because of the conditions mentioned before, and many more could be added, and thus they complain and murmur. What happened to the children of Israel because they murmured and were afraid and complained? They had so little faith. They forgot that God had safely brought them thus far and He could also lead them and protect them the rest of the way to the promised land. Thus many of them did not get to enter, only Joshua and Caleb and the younger generation. We too are looking forward to a promised land. Are we going to become bitter and die, or are we going to trust in the Lord, that He will safely lead us through these trying times?

Also in the interpretation we should include that His voice, "the sound of many waters," this time bitter waters because of sin, is warning us that the day of judgment is approaching. Isn't God giving man time to *repent?* Many will not, so to them it means death, a separation from God, here and in eternity.

What was the *shadowy or thin cloud through which could be seen other objects or things behind it.* REV 8:13: "And I beheld, and heard an angel flying through the midst of heaven, saying with a loud voice, Woe, woe, woe, to the inhabiters of the earth by reason of the other voices of the trumpet of the three angels, which are yet to sound!" The shadowy objects, then, are the other judgments that are yet to come.

And the *bomb?* We all know that there shall be wars and rumors of wars before the end. God's word says so. In the vision the bomb was moving across the path of the four-star square. It was moving. This puzzled me at the time, and there was no interpretation until some time later, in October of the same year, 1973. But there was a vision before that, in August of 1973, which I also did not understand until October. So let us consider it first.

FROGS

This happened on the night of August 19, 1973, another vision. As I went into the kitchen, I saw a roaster on the range top. But I wasn't cooking, or roasting anything. Starting toward the stove, I hesitated slightly, because there, in the center of the range top, heads turned toward the roaster, were two large frogs with men's eyes. Now they stared at me. After hesitating, I went forward and took the lid from the roaster. There was the most perfectly baked chicken I had ever seen. Oh, so perfectly baked, golden brown, but between each wing and the body sat a frog, and down between the legs sat another frog. Yes, three frogs were **inside** the roaster, all with men's eyes. I quickly put the lid on and walked away. Again I woke up.

What was this all about? I remembered that there was something in the Bible about three frogs, but where? As soon as possible I went for my Bible. Yes, there it was, REV 16:13–14: "And I saw three unclean spirits like frogs come out of the mouth of the dragon, and out of the mouth of the beast, and out of the mouth of the false prophet. For they are the spirits of devils, working miracles, which go forth unto the kings of the earth and of the whole world, to gather them to the battle of that great day of God Almighty." Is this Armageddon?

Halley's Bible Handbook puts it this way: "Battle lines being drawn for Armageddon. The dragon, satan; the beast, world government; the false prophet, the apostate church, all in alliance." End of quote. Even as far back as 1965, when the twenty-fourth edition was written, Halley explained it thus. Does someone ask, "How can he say the apostate church?" Page 733 says:

> Even in our country, where we think we have the purest form of Christianity known, since the day of primitive persecutions, while there are vast multitude of devoted saints, and countless True and Faithful churches, seminaries, organizations and movements, headed by pastors and leaders of unwavering loyalty and unquestioned faith, yet, on the other hand our churches generally are so thoroughly humanized, so full of worldliness, indifference, heartlessness, pleasure seeking: all kinds of evil indulgence, so much unbelief in the pulpit and in Seminaries, so little of God's Word in the preaching, so little of Christ in the services, so much lifeless formalism, so much professionalism and ecclesiastical pomp, so little of the

real spirit of Christ, so much ignorance of God's Word, and such indifference to it in the pulpit. All this makes it look as if the church as a whole has not yet come entirely out of the GREAT APOSTASY.*

In REV 2–3 we read *seven* times: "He that hath an ear let him hear what the Spirit saith unto the churches." Notice it is plural, *churches.* And in the vision I was shown that the last one is *lukewarm.*

Besides the three frogs in the roaster there were also two frogs on the range top. There must also be another interpretation of the vision. It wasn't until October that this part was revealed and understood. Another war, so that was the bomb in my other vision. The perfectly baked chicken was Israel. God has prepared for Himself a people. The three frogs (with men's eyes) who were trying to take over were Syria, Egypt, and Jordan. The two big frogs were Russia and the U.S.A. sitting by, watching to see what was going to happen and ready also to jump into the trouble. I quickly put the lid on; thus, for the time being, the lid is on the trouble. They are still eyeing each other, and anything can happen. Are you watching? **WHAT TIME IS IT?** Are you praying and ready for that great day when Jesus is coming again, this time to take His own unto himself, *but* also the terrible judgment on all those who neglected His word and word hearers only, but not doers of the same? Let me repeat MAT 7:21: "NOT EVERY ONE THAT SAYETH UNTO ME LORD, LORD, SHALL ENTER INTO THE KINGDOM OF HEAVEN; BUT HE THAT DOETH THE WILL OF MY FATHER WHICH IS IN HEAVEN." LUK 6:46: "And why call ye me, Lord, Lord, and do not the things which I say?"

---

* *Halley's Bible Handbook,* p. 733. Copyright 1965. Used by permission.

DON'T WAKE HIM UP

Don't wake him up. Yes I had heard it, but for some reason or other, I just didn't think much about it. I had even answered, "I think he is already awake." But then by October 1974 I became very disturbed, restless, and more and more puzzled. Why? There I had seen those visions and had those dreams, and they were going through my mind over and over again. What, if anything, was I to do about them?

Going to town the week of Halloween didn't help any, but seemed to make matters worse. Yes, already the Christmas decorations and displays with Santa Claus were in the store windows. *Oh, no, not already,* was my thought. Such commercialism! This was going just too far. Wasn't it high time to do or say something? But what?

During the forty-mile ride home, one plan after another came to mind. Finally I decided that I needed some help, some advice from someone. But who? Now there was a pastor that I thought might understand and give me the help and advice that I needed. I played around with that thought for several days. Would he be interested? Would he understand, or would he take it lightly and say, "Just another dream"? Over and over again, I wondered how he would receive it if I sent a brief outline of the visions to him. Somehow I felt, time and again, though, that only God could give me the proper guidance, because only *His will should be done.* He knew the truth and that there had been visions and dreams. So after several days, I prayed, "Dear Heavenly Father, You know how disturbed I have been, and I don't know what to do. You know how often I fail and the mistakes that I make, so I come to You for help and guidance. I don't want to do anything against Thy will or to mislead anyone. Because I know that Thy word has an answer to every problem. I pray that Thou would guide and lead me to what You would have me to do. I shall open my Bible and read what is in the lower right hand corner of the right hand page. Take Thou my hand and lead me, Thy will be done. Amen."

I took the Bible that I usually carry only to church and opened it. There was the answer. HAB 1:–4: "O LORD, how long shall I cry, and thou wilt not hear! even cry out unto thee of violence, and thou wilt not save! Why dost thou shew me iniquity, and cause me to behold grievance? for spoiling and violence are before me: and there are that raise up strife and contention. Therefore the law is slacked, and judgment doth never go forth: for the wicked doth compass about the righteous; therefore wrong judgment proceedeth."

Continuing in HAB 2:1–4: "I will stand upon my watch, and set me upon the tower, and will watch to see what he will say unto me, and what I shall answer when I am reproved. And the LORD answered me, and said, Write the vision, and make it plain upon tables, that he may run that readeth it. For the vision is yet for an appointed time, but at the end it shall speak, and not lie: though it tarry, wait for it; because it will surely come, it will not tarry. Behold, his soul which is lifted up is not upright in him: but the just shall live by his faith."

So I wrote to this pastor. Whether he answered it or his secretary I don't know. The answer: "God did sometimes speak to people in visions." He would suggest that I daily read God's word and go to Him daily in prayer. I must let Him be my Lord and Savior. (I had been doing that for many, many years.) Now what should I do?

My plan had failed. There was no advice or encouragement about the visions, even though I had asked what he would do. Why? Why? Hadn't I prayed and asked

God for guidance? Then, wonders of wonders, *He had answered my prayer.* Had I so quickly forgotten that voice from heaven and that command: *"Don't wake him up"*? Who, the MINISTRY, the CLERGY, the man I had seen in the vision, dozing in the recliner?

But I had prayed for guidance and read that Scripture again. How wonderful it was when I did. HAB 2:2: "Write it on tables that he may run that readeth it." Wait, yes, I read it again. There was the answer. There was where I had failed. It did not say write it in a *letter* that he may read. It said "write the vision, and make it plain *upon tables,* that he may run that readeth it." It was plural, yes, *tables, books.* It was not to be for one person, but for whoever would read it.

Thus we see again how carefully, thoughtfully, we should read the Scriptures and apply them. Just as mentioned previously, even those little words, "but," "if," "is," "what," et cetera, are very, very important. Have we been ignoring them to some extent, not taking them seriously enough, to let our thoughts dwell on them as we read them?

I had failed to grasp the whole meaning of what I had read. My thoughts, evidently, were on what I planned to do, and so I had failed to fully grasp what *God* wanted *ME* to do. Remember how during the vision of the stars I heard *Don't wake him up?* I answered, "I think that he is already awake." Have you read David Alsobrook's booklet *Awake Church?* He explains about a dozing ministry.

It wasn't until the vision and interpretation of the dozing man and the kneeling woman that the blinders fell from my eyes. Step by step, each part of REV 3:15–18 was brought to my mind, and I had to ask myself, "Why does the church think it is rich? Why is it poor, blind, miserable, and naked?" So, by the guidance of the Holy

Spirit, little by little the reasons were brought to my attention and remembrance. Now what was I to do about it? Uneducated as I am, I was plainly shown, by what you have read, *write it on tables* that *all* may run that read it.

THE SHAKING FIST AND TEARS

It is November 1974. After going to bed about nine-thirty that night, I woke up because my feet were itching, and I heard: *Itching feet.* I repeated it: "Itching feet." Then I heard: *Eyes wide open.* I repeated it: "Eyes wide open," and again, and each time thereafter, I repeated what I heard. Then I saw an arm raised to the sky, and a fist was shaking, as if in anger. There was also a face, brimming over with tears. "Such tears," I said. Never before had I seen such tears.

Now the shadowy figure that I had seen several times before appeared, leading a young man dressed in black and a young woman dressed in white. I said, "I can't remember it all." Now there was a can, like a shortening can, and I heard and repeated, "Can." Then: *Get up and write.* I answered, "It is too cold." Then: *Turn on the body heat.* Now I replied, "All right, I'll get up and write."

I was really wide awake and so got up and went into the family room and to my desk. I wrote down all that I had seen and heard. *Oh, I forgot eyes wide open,* I thought. As I looked at the top of the list, there it was. I had written it down, and I heard: *Arafat, Arafat, Arafat.* Yes, three times. Now I was shivering. I was cold, but I also think I was shivering because of what I had heard and seen. I hurried to bed, but not to sleep. Immediately I seemed to understand what the shaking fist and the face with all those tears were to tell me. Nothing is hidden from God. He sees and knows how sinful man has become. Remember how He said, at the time of Noah, "I will not always strive with man"? His anger is truly kindled. The *face with all the tears,* that reminds us how Jesus wept over Jerusalem (LUK 19:41–44). Wasn't he weeping in this vision because He had so loved the world that He suffered, and died that man might have forgiveness of sins, but now, because man has rejected this love and grace and mercy, the terrible judgments that had been prophesied were about to take place. Ah, there it is: *Itching feet,* that shows God's readiness for action. God's eyes have been wide open. His feet are ready to go forward, to carry out what had been prophesied. The shadowy figure, then, is the Holy Spirit or angel, safely leading God's children and protecting them.

Can, yes, I was to remember it, and then, so that I surely would not forget, or probably also that others should know about **what is about to happen,** I was told to get up and write. I did. Thinking that I had forgotten eyes wide open and checking to be sure that I had written it down and at the same time hearing: *Arafat, Arafat, Arafat,* I believe shows that we are to be wide awake to what Arafat and the P.L.O. are doing.

As I am writing this, there has already been the meeting at Camp David and so many talks since, but no agreement. We have also heard that Arafat said that there would be no peace until his people are restored to what he called their homeland. Since then, in November 1988, Arafat was denied a visa to the United States to visit and address the U.N. He has visited several countries since and has already made three visits to the pope. Are you watching? All happenings are pointing strongly to REV 13. *What time is it?* Are you prepared?

BUMPETY BUMP

It is Friday, September 28, 1977. Before going to bed I read JER 50 and 51. After praying for wisdom and a better understanding of what I had read, I put the Bible aside. Sitting there for a while and meditating on the things I had read and thinking about the visions and dreams and that I was doing nothing much about them, I became somewhat depressed. Then I prayed, "Dear Heavenly Father, I know that Your word has an answer to every problem, and so I pray, again, for guidance and direction from You. Guide me thus in the reading of Thy word. Amen." Reaching over and again picking up my Bible, I opened it, and near my hand was the answer. "Woman, what have I to do with thee? My hour is not yet come" (JOH 2:4). What an answer! I was trying to rush ahead of Him. Then I thought, *Yes, remember Mary went to the servants AND TOLD THEM TO DO WHATSOEVER HE SAID.* It wasn't long before Jesus also went to the servants and told them to fill the water pots with water and the water was changed to wine. She did prepare the way to an understanding, a willingness for them to obey Jesus' command.

Many, many things will happen before the Lord comes; some of them are prophesied in His word. I am yet a scholar in the school of preparation, but the wonderful ways in which I am taught these lessons also teaches me of the power of the Holy Spirit. *Praise and thanks be unto God.*

WOMAN ON THE TRACKS

A woman a little taller than I and I were leaving a large gathering of people. She was pushing a large box or chest on wheels ahead of her down the railroad bed between the tracks. I had an armful of things wrapped in a cloth and was walking a little ahead of her outside the tracks. Looking ahead, I commented about the holiday appearance of the town just ahead of us on the right hand side. When we reached the place, we crossed over and onto the sidewalk. There were only soldiers all along the left side, lined up, shoulder to shoulder, each holding a gun pointing upward. On the right hand side were places of business, banks, et cetera. I didn't look right or left, just straight ahead. Finally we reached the corner.

The woman, pushing this box or chest ahead of her, rushed past me and crossed the street. Now she stepped up onto the sidewalk, passed the first house, and then turned around the left side of it. I said, "We're on the wrong side of the house." I thought, *What would the people think if they should look out their window and see us here?* The woman turned about and went back to the corner and then down the middle of the street. I got ahead of her. A girl about eight to ten years old was coming up the street screaming, holding her hands over her ears. She stopped, picked up a large flower and a bow that must have fallen from a flower arrangement, and then started screaming again. By that time we were even with her. The woman said to her, "Everything is going to be all right; here's the key." Thus saying, she pushed the key between the girl's lips. Of course that stopped her screaming.

After going a little farther, we saw a backyard to the right of us partially covered with torn, broken floral arrangements. As we went farther down the street, flowers and bows were strewn along the way and in the gutters. There, in a yard to the left of us, were three caskets in a row. In the yard next door there was another one; then in the third yard, there were two caskets, one beside the other. As we got to the first yard, I remembered who lived there. Two of them had been dead for several years. I also remembered who lived in the third place, and they are still living. Going down the street, which was somewhat hilly, we finally reached the other corner. I had seen a large field ahead of us. Four corner posts marked it off, forming an oblong field. I said, "Maybe we had better go around it; he may have something planted there." As we reached the back side of the field, there was something ahead of us, something like an old streetcar, but it was partly submerged; we could only see part of it. It opened from the rear. As we entered it, I said, "Well, we will have light and heat here." We went in. There were other people there. The woman was gone. I never saw her again. Seats were lengthwise along the wall, just like the old streetcars. A few people were sitting there.

A girl about eight to ten years old came from the other end and flopped across a footrest or hassock. I didn't know what to do and stood there with my bundle. I noticed a comfortable chair to the left of the entrance, a large plant, and something like a palm at the left of the chair. It was the only comfortable chair in sight. Surely I shouldn't take that. But then the people seemed to be going down to the other end. "Well, if I'm going to be knitting for them, the light will be best there, and so I had better take the chair," I said. Going toward it, I woke up.

Symbols and Their Meanings
1. Woman and me: Church and I leaving a worldly situation.
2. She rolls ahead of her a chest on wheels: Burdens or worldly matters that the church wants to cling to.
3. My small bundle: Faith, hope, and love, the most precious possessions of a Christian.

4. Bumpety bump: Makes for rough travel when trying to carry on so much of the *busy-ness* of churches today.
5. Walking outside the track: Walking a smoother, safer way with Jesus.
6. See the city ahead: Both look forward to the city of God, New Jerusalem.
7. Soldiers on one side of the sidewalk, businesses on the other: The government and the world, also worldliness.
8. Pass through them but cross the street: Christians must pass through them but are headed for a better destination.
9. The woman crosses the street and goes up the other sidewalk and around the house: The church sometimes crosses over, accepting some of the ways of the world.
10. I draw her attention to the error: True Christians should do so.
11. She returns to the right way: Christians accept admonitions.
12. Screaming child coming toward us: Restless, questioning youth.
13. Woman pushes key into her mouth: Saying the church has the answers.
14. "Everything is going to be all right": Peace, peace, when there is no peace.
15. Strewn flowers and bows, et cetera: Things of this world, scattered by the whirlwind of God's anger.
16. Unburied caskets: As prophesied, that in the last days the dead shall not be buried.
17. Large open field, marked off by posts:?
18. Conveyance, partly hidden or underground: As the end of our journey nears, the church will be partially driven underground.

19. Woman disappears: Seeks the deeper shelter.
20. Child flopped across a hassock or footrest: Feels the safety and rest provided at the feet of God.
21. Chair near the door, plant, and light: Someone will take it; should I? An urge made me do so, to knit together all the promises of God's word, here shown by the green plant, and because it is light, we will all need the light of God's words and promises of His grace, protection, and blessings.

Now let us put it all together. God is not leaving us in the dark. He is preparing and warning us of some of the things that are yet to happen. I thought about all that dream, and then I seemed to feel so tired, but was God, by the power of the Holy Spirit, trying to tell me something, show me something? It was all so plain, all those details but oh, I was so tired. Then I prayed, "Dear Heavenly Father, is there a message in this dream for me? Do You want me to accept it as a message from You? There is so much to it, and I am so tired. What is Thy will? Your will be done." I must have gone right to sleep and even slept overtime.

That dream was so fresh in my mind the next night, when I was getting ready to go to bed, that after my evening prayers I prayed again, if there be a message for me in that dream, that God would unfold it for me. I prayed for guidance, wisdom, and understanding. There was no sleep. It all went through my mind again. Well, if I would just start at the very beginning, take it step by step, take each things as I saw it, then I would soon know.

Thus first, *all the people that we were leaving* . . . the people of the world all about us. The church was generally pictured as a woman, so she would be the church. I was the person outside the organized church, at present, but attending services regularly.

The woman pushing the large chest or box ahead of her is the church. REV 3:17: "Because thou sayest, I am rich, and increased with goods, and have need of nothing; and knowest not that thou art wretched, and miserable, and poor, and blind, and naked." Yes, she had a whole chest full of things, no doubt that she cherished and wanted to keep, to save. I was most likely carrying a few necessary belongings tied up in a cloth. She was pushing her things, *bumpety bump, over the railroad ties . . .* all the added activities of the organized church, bazaars, puppet shows, so many meetings, retreats, conferences, ever learning and so little time to apply what they have learned.

I was *walking smoothly along the outside of the tracks.* God was smoothing out the way ahead of me; it even lightened what I was carrying. I had time to look about and to look ahead and to observe what was happening as we traveled along. We both turned when we got to town and went up onto the sidewalk. We were traveling the same road together. All those soldiers to the left were the government; to the right the bank and places of business were the world. The government and the financial world, worldly business, were fencing us in. As we reached the corner, she pushed across the street, ahead of me, and in her hurry she passed the place where she should have turned. So intent was she on what she was doing that she missed the right way that she should go. She *missed the right way,* just as many churches do today. Yes, I went along, BUT DID DIRECT HER ATTENTION TO WHAT SHE HAD DONE, just as I have often spoken up when things were being said or done that did not seem to go along with God's word. *She didn't say a word,* just as so many church people today resent when things are brought to their attention. But sometimes it works, and so we get back on the right road, just as we did in the dream.

The *screaming child* is youth, wondering, *Why all the chaos and trouble in the world?* Why is the national debt rising higher and higher, and they will have to pay, and already, there are so many of them having such a difficult time in life to get started? Some people have been unemployed for so long. Church members, so many of them rich, how did they earn their money? Many are living in luxury while people around have only the bare necessities.

The woman saying, "Everything is going to be all right," is not as the Bible tells us. The Bible says: "PEACE, PEACE, WHEN THERE IS NO PEACE" (JER 6:14 and JER 8:11). *Pushing the key between her lips to silence her* was the church saying, "We have the key, the answer to the problems."

The yard with all the broken up floral offerings, these are the earthly things of this world that shall perish, even as we saw, along the street and gutters, bows and flowers no doubt scattered by the winds of God's wrath because of sin.

Next we passed those three yards. The first had three caskets in it, the second had one, and the third had two caskets, sitting right there in the open. Now that was a puzzle, I just did not understand it at the time. *But* on the night of October 27, 1977, a month after the dream, which was on September 28, I woke up during the early morning hours and could not go back to sleep. Finally I prayed, "Dear Heavenly Father, if You have something to say to me or to bring to my attention, I'll be glad to stay awake. . . . Your will be done."

I did not go back to sleep, but instead the dream with the strewn flowers and torn and scattered floral arrangements and those caskets sitting out there in the open in those yards came back to my mind. Well, hadn't I read something about the dead not being buried? Sure, that is in JER 25, where the ruin of all nations is foretold. I'll quote two verses of it here. JER 25:32–33: "Thus saith the LORD of hosts, Behold, evil shall go forth from nation to nation, and a GREAT WHIRLWIND SHALL BE RAISED UP FROM THE COASTS OF THE EARTH." (The bows and flowers and floral offerings scattered everywhere, as seen in the dream.) Verse 33: "And the slain of the LORD shall be at that day from one end of the earth even unto the other end of the earth: they shall not be lamented, neither gathered, nor buried; they shall be dung upon the ground." There was no one near the caskets, nor were they gathered into a funeral home, and they were not buried. Now doesn't that make you tremble? It does me. Wasn't that giving me the interpretation of the things that I had seen in the dream, *and the whirlwind? Has one of the winds that the angels were holding back already been released,* as shown me in the vision about the four winds? What time is it? Are we prepared? Yes, what time *is* it?

Going down the hilly street and seeing the open field, true, we should not trespass. God has laid out a way for us; we should follow that. Going will be a lot easier if we let God have His way, if we accept His will. He will lead us to a safe refuge; as I said during the dream, "It will be light and warm here." The light of His word and the warmth of his love will be with us. The child also rested her head on the footstool and found rest; youth also can feel secure here.

The chair near the door? I didn't think I was entitled to use it. What was this? It was God's comforting guidance. Here he would make it possible for me to knit for them, put together the long thread of God's word for them, when it seemed this place was partly underground. We shall probably be driven underground to some extent by the conditions during those final days.

The Fourth Trumpet

OTHER DREAMS

There have been other dreams, the Food Series, dating back to the early seventies and three or four which occurred in 1977. At the time, I paid little attention to them. What seems strange, though, is that they are, to some extent, still fresh in my mind. The Food Series is only mentioned here without comments. Three dreams from 1977, "Lights," "Follow Me," and "The Clock," are recorded with interpretations.

Food Series
Briefly, the family and friends had been invited for a dinner. The table was laden with so many good things to eat. Some weeks later, I had a dream in which only the family had been invited and there was not the variety of food that we had at the previous meal. In another dream, there was only one large bowl of food for all. In another, a man dressed in black knocked at the door. I opened it, he entered; and sat down in a chair in the kitchen. Not a word was spoken. I just opened the refrigerator door and showed him that it was empty, so he got up and left.

Lights
In one dream, *only the lights in three rooms, then two, and finally only one light in the house could be turned on. The switches just wouldn't work. Only one light in the*

house was workable, and I just could not understand it.

Energy crisis? What if this terrible coal strike continues? Some power companies are already low on coal. God only knows the answers. Now what about Iran causing the oil shortage? I truly believe that the energy problems are warnings of troubles to come. Why? Has the fourth trumpet sounded? Let us read what the Bible says about it. REV 8:12: "And the fourth angel sounded, and the third part of the sun was smitten, and the third part of the moon, and the third part of the stars; so as the third part of them was darkened, and the day shone not for a third part of it, and the night likewise." Isn't this again symbolic or probably both symbolic and literal?

Because one-third part of the sun, moon, and stars was smitten or one-third of the Pure Light, there will be a decline in the availability of God's Holy Word. God is permitting it to happen. Why? Just as we read in ISA 5:30: "And in that day they shall roar against them like the roaring of the sea: and if one look unto the land, behold darkness and sorrow, and the light is darkened in the heavens thereof." A picture of judgments.

A prophecy in the Old Testament, AMO 8, is a picture of world conditions, very much like the present-day world which will lead to a drought of His word. Verses 9 and 11 say: "And it shall come to pass in that day, saith the Lord GOD, that I will cause the sun to go down at noon, and I will darken the earth in the clear day" and "Behold, the days come, saith the Lord GOD, that I will send a famine in the land, not a famine of bread, nor a thirst for water, BUT OF HEARING THE WORDS OF THE LORD."

The New Testament warns (MAT 24:11–12): "And many false prophets shall rise, and shall deceive many. And because iniquity shall abound, the love of many shall wax cold." Isn't it happening all around us? As we heard when the third trumpet sounded. Bitter words have turned many to bitterness. Check the church attendance, the Sunday School and Bible Class attendance, and you will find that only about one-half of those listed as members are attending. Why? Isn't the *light* in so *many* instances fading out? Thus the energy crisis fading out of the light makes it seem that the fourth trumpet has blown. It was prophesied that it would happen. Read what Jesus Himself said, in MAT 24:24–27, "For there shall arise false Christs, and false prophets, and shall shew great signs and wonders; insomuch that, if it were possible, they shall deceive the very elect. Behold, I have told you before. Wherefore if they shall say unto you, Behold, he is in the desert; go not forth: behold, he is in the secret chambers; believe it not. For as the lightning cometh out of the east, and shineth even unto the west; so shall also the coming of the Son of man be."

The prophecy of REV 8:12 speaks of one-third of the sun, moon, and stars being smitten. The light of God's Word is being darkened by all kinds of cults arising and rapidly increasing. Isn't God allowing it because of the hardness of men's hearts? Then what follows? REV 8:13: "And I beheld, and heard an angel flying through the midst of heaven, saying with a loud voice, Woe, woe, woe, to the inhabiters of the earth by reason of the other voices of the trumpet of the three angels, which are yet to sound!"

Follow Me

A dream that remains vivid in my mind—I cannot forget it—is included here because it gave me confidence. The Holy Spirit seemed to be leading me to write about its revelations to me.

We were riding on something that at first seemed like a bus or streetcar. We arrived at a brightly lit town. I wanted to get off and rang the bell, but the driver kept right on going. He said that he was not allowed to stop in the city. When we did stop and I was getting off, it seemed more like getting off the rear end of a truck. A man helped me to get my things together; he jumped down and then helped me down. Then he handed me an umbrella and said, "You may need this." He then picked up an umbrella, but it seemed more like a shepherd's crook, and now he followed behind me. After we had gone several yards, he came forward and said, "Follow me," and walked on ahead. I had been guided by the lights of the city, but then I followed him. Suddenly he jumped down an embankment, stopped, and waited for me. I told him that I couldn't jump down that far and started to walk around the embankment. A man was coming up the incline. I told him that I was sorry to have to cross his property, and he answered, "It is okay. Be careful, though; there is some water down there, and you may get your feet wet." Soon I met the first man and he started ahead again. Following him for a short distance, I then went around a corner, and there before us was the city. The man suddenly disappeared. There were stores on both sides of the street. I hadn't gone very far when I was at and in a strange house.

There were a number of people in the dining-living room combination. A girl about nine or ten years old was sitting at the far end of the room reading. There was a loud knock at the door. When I went to answer it, there was no one there. At a table in the middle of the street right in front of the house a number of men were drinking and playing cards. Another girl tried to rush past me. I called her back.

She said, "I'm going to play with—"

I didn't get the name but said to her, "No you are not, because she is in the house reading. Come back."

She did.

Turning to go back into the house, I noticed that the mail had not been taken in and commented, "They even forgot to take in the mail." Then, as I was getting the mail from the box, there seemed to be so much of it, each time that I took some into the house I had to go back for more. Now there were even packages there, and I sure was puzzled. Finally the mailbox was empty, but the dining room table was piled high with mail: letters, boxes, honeydew melons, oranges, et cetera. Puzzled, yes, how could all that come from that mailbox? Standing there, looking at all the things on the table, was also the first man that had said, "Follow me." Now he said, "Better lock the door." I went to do so, but couldn't, because the lock was a poor fit. Looking at it and wondering what to do, I heard something. Looking upward toward the ceiling, I noticed a heavy metal wall and door coming down from above. They were going between us and the wooden door with the ill-fitting lock. People were trying to break down the door, and it seemed to shatter, but the metal wall stopped them. Trembling, I stepped backward and then started to go even farther back into the room, but beside me, again, stood the same man that had said, "Follow me," and, "Better lock the door." This time, smiling, he said, "All will be all right." There was no more fear, and I woke up.

Now, with the guidance of the Holy Spirit, I shall endeavor to give you the interpretation of this dream. I was traveling, going somewhere. Yes, life is a journey. "For here we have no continuing city, but we seek the one to come" (HEB 13:14). *We were nearing the city, my destination, but the driver was not allowed to stop in the city.* Here we have the world trying to mislead us, take us off our course away from eternal security and a life with God.

Finally he stopped. A man, unknown to me, helped me down. He offered me protection, symbolized by the umbrella and his words: "You may need this." Then he took something like an *umbrella, but more like a shepherd's crook, and said, "Follow me; I'll show you the way."* How wonderful. Jesus, my Savior, had said, "Follow me; I'll show you the way."

When the man jumped down the embankment, I could not follow. Our path of life is not always level and easy, but if Jesus is leading us, we should follow in all faith, knowing we'll be safe in His care. But I didn't follow. Just as an example, I would discontinue writing. As I walked around the embankment, so I tried getting around what I had started and wanted to do, but then went my way. Then as I do so, I get the warning: "There is water down there; be careful and don't get your feet wet." In other words: "You decided to go your way; it could lead you into trouble."

Only the love and guidance of God could lead me back to the true shepherd, and now there He was, and He safely led me on, around the corner, and into the city. This was not my final destination, though. *There are businesses all along the street,* the world. NOW *I am suddenly near, then inside a house. Other people are also there.* These must be other Christians whom God has also led here for safety reasons. The *knock on the door?* The world—some would like to enter on their own terms also.

The girl trying to run out represents those that God called, brought to safety, into the fold, but who want to cling to worldly pleasures. The *other girl, reading,* is those that are content in the safety and guidance of God.

Now: "They haven't even taken in the mail." What about that? Even many of those that we think are secure in God's house, the church, are so often slack in taking in His letters to them, His word. But He is ever faithful and provides, just as was shown by all the mail, boxes, and fruit that was piled upon the dining room table. When we really, faithfully, partake of His word, He richly blesses us and gives us more and more abundantly.

Thus *I took it in and placed it upon the table; it was for all of us.* Isn't this a lesson for me? Even as I called back and reproved the girl that wanted to slip out to worldly pleasures, why and how should I do such? Because He had said, "Follow me; I'll show you the way." So all this writing must also be entrusted to the guidance of God, His will be done. After it is written, completed, then what? He'll show me the way, even though it all seems so uncertain now. "Follow me," he said.

The man appears again and tells me to lock the door. But the lock is so imperfect it will not lock. All our righteousness is so imperfect. Now how wonderful! The *new wall and the heavy door* come between us and the world. Jesus said as we read in JOH 10:7–11: "Then said Jesus unto them again, Verily, verily, I say unto you, I am the door of the sheep. All that ever came before me are thieves and robbers: but the sheep did not hear them. I am the door: by me if any man enter in, he shall be saved, and shall go in and out, and find pasture. The thief cometh not, but for to steal, and to kill, and to destroy: I am come that they might have life, and that they might have it more abundantly. I am the good shepherd: the good shepherd giveth his life for the sheep." ISA 26:20–21: "Come, my people, enter thou into thy chambers, and shut thy doors about thee: hide thyself as it were for a little moment, until the indignation be overpast. For, behold, the LORD cometh out of his place to punish the inhabitants of the earth for their iniquity: the earth also shall disclose her blood, and shall no more cover her slain."

"Follow me," He says to His own. ARE YOU FOLLOWING HIM, PREPARED? WHAT TIME IS IT?

The Clock

It is November 1, 1977. My husband and I woke up early, probably because we had just gone back onto standard time. We lay in each other's arms for a few minutes, but then decided to go back to sleep. It was only 5:50 A.M. I turned over toward the wall, thanking God for my hubby and the fifty-seven years of a happy life together. I had just about gone to sleep when I heard: *The clock shall be taken away.* I chimed in and said, "And there shall be time no more." Thus I admitted that I knew what had been said. I turned back to my husband and told him what had happened. He said, "We'll watch and wait for Him." If the clock is taken away *it would mean that no one had any more time, just* as I had chimed in, "And there shall be time no more." But now what shall we think? What shall we say? We have read those words before. *Where?* REV 10:5–6: "And the angel which I saw stand upon the sea and upon the earth lifted up his hand to heaven, And sware by him that liveth for ever and ever, who created heaven, and the things that therein are, and the earth, and the things that therein are, and the sea, and the things which are therein, THAT THERE SHOULD BE TIME NO LONGER." Oh, dear reader, are we that close to the end, when there will be no more time to prepare? Are we prepared? Jesus says, as we read in REV 3:20, "Behold, I stand at the door, and knock: if any man hear my voice, and open the door, I will come in to him, and will sup with him, and he with me." He said this almost two thousand year ago. Aren't we thus that much closer? Oh, He has been so patient!

MAT 24:36–39: "But of that day and hour knoweth no man, no, not the angels of heaven, but my Father only. But as the days of Noe were, so shall also the coming of the Son of man be. For as in the days that were before the flood they were eating and drinking, marrying and giving in marriage, until the day that Noe entered into the ark, And knew not until the flood came, and took them all away; so shall also the coming of the Son of man be."

In MAR 13:32–37 we read:

> But of that day and that hour knoweth no man, no, not the angels which are in heaven, neither the Son, but the Father. Take ye heed, watch and pray: for ye know not when the time is. For the Son of Man is as a man taking a far journey, who left his house, and gave authority to his servants, and to every man his work, and commanded the porter to watch. Watch ye therefore: for ye know not when the master of the house cometh, at even, or at midnight, or at the cockcrowing, or in the morning: Lest coming suddenly he find you sleeping. And what I say unto you I say unto all, Watch.

REV 22:7: "Behold, I come quickly: blessed is he that keepeth the sayings of the prophecy of this book." REV 22:12–13 and 16: "And, behold, I come quickly; and my reward is with me, to give every man according as his work shall be. I am Alpha and Omega, the beginning and the end, the first and the last" and "I Jesus have sent mine angel to testify unto you these things in the churches. I am the root and the offspring of David, and the bright and morning star." READ IT AGAIN: "I, JESUS, HAVE SENT MINE ANGEL TO TESTIFY *UNTO YOU THESE THINGS IN THE CHURCHES*. I am the root and the offspring of David, and the bright and morning star."

With God, there is no straddling the fence; in His sight we are either hot or cold. If we are *lukewarm he will spue us out of his mouth.* In the first book of the New Testament, He speaks of two classes of people, as we read in MAT

25:34, 37, and 41: the "righteous" ("blessed of my Father") and the "cursed." In the last book of the New Testament we read of two classes of people, in REV 21:7, 8, and 21: "the nations of them which are saved" ("he that overcometh") and the "unbelieving." What a terrible judgment on those that we read about in verse 8: "But the fearful, and unbelieving, and the abominable, and murderers, and whoremongers, and sorcerers, and idolaters, and all liars, shall have their part in the lake which burneth with fire and brimstone: which is the second death." How terrible, eternal separation from God.

How wonderful, however, are the following words, REV 21: 1–7:

> And I saw a new heaven and a new earth: for the first heaven and the first earth were passed away; and there was no more sea. And I John saw the holy city, new Jerusalem, coming down from God out of heaven, prepared as a bride adorned for her husband. And I heard a great voice out of heaven saying, Behold, the tabernacle of God is with men, and he will dwell with them, and they shall be his people, and God himself shall be with them, and be their God. And God shall wipe away all tears from their eyes; and there shall be no more death, neither sorrow, nor crying, neither shall there be any more pain: for the former things are passed away. And he that sat upon the throne said, Behold, I make all things new. And he said unto me, Write: for these words are true and faithful. And he said unto me, It is done. I am Alpha and Omega, the beginning and the end. I will give unto him that is athirst of the fountain of the water of life freely. He that overcometh shall inherit all things; and I will be his God, and he shall be my son.

Verse 20, chapter 22, of Revelations: "HE WHICH TESTIFIETH THESE THINGS SAITH,

SURELY, I COME QUICKLY.
Amen. Even so, come, Lord Jesus."

Let Us Ever Walk

Let us ever walk with Jesus,
Follow His example pure,
Flee the world that would deceive us
And to sin our souls allure.
Ever in His footsteps treading,
Body here, yet soul above,
Full of faith and hope and love,
Let us do the Father's bidding.
Faithful Lord, abide with me.
Savior, lead. I follow thee.

Epilogue

It is Friday morning, November 30/December 1, 1989, and I just must type out what happened on the night of the thirtieth. After all these years there has been another vision.

I was standing on a sidewalk with a number of people when I realized that I wasn't properly dressed but was partly naked. Trying to decide on what to do, I was being swept ahead by the people.

As we reached a large department store the doors opened and we all went in. How strange, all the clerks were sitting behind the counters. During all the past years they had to stand there.

We browsed around some and then followed the crowd down the center aisle.

Suddenly a woman that was leaning against the counter tapped me on the shoulder and asked, "Did you find the book for him that you were looking for?"

I answered, "Yes, I did."

A woman just in front of me asked, "Did you know her?"

"Yes," I answered. "I've known her for a good many years."

We were nearing the back of the store. There in front of us, up against the wall, was a really large clock that almost reached the ceiling. It was old and it looked as if a panel were breaking away from it. There were heavy weights hanging from under the face of it. The largest weight now seemed to move slowly.

I was in the front row of all these people, but in front of me, on table after table, were coffee cakes. Oh, so pretty. I wondered how they were going to distribute them. Then one caught my eye. Oh, so pretty, caramel topping with plenty of nuts. Two pieces had already been cut from it. I hoped that I could have that one. Then I awoke.

Interpretation

Standing on a sidewalk: God's path laid out for us.
Not properly dressed: I too am a sinner.
Trying to decide on what to do: Realizing my condition.
Being swept away with the others: All have sinned.
Large department store: God's storehouse.
Doors open: God's invitation to come in. We all went in.
Clerks sitting behind the counters: Halfheartedness.
We browse around: We are looking things over.
Woman leaning against the counter: The church.
"Did you find the book for him?" "Yes, I did": the pastors.
"Did you know her?" "Yes, I did": I've been a church member all my life.
Back of the store: Can go no further.
Clock against the back of the store: God upholds and controls the clock.
A panel about to break away: Earthly time will soon end.
In front of the people: I too am old.
Small, round individual tables: God has prepared for each of us.
A coffee cake on each one: Breakfast food. A new day is dawning.

How will they distribute them?: The heavenly Father will do so.

Two pieces are gone from such a perfect one: I hope that I can have that one. I have already tasted God's love and mercy and grace.